Discovering Biblical Treasures

UNDERSTANDING ESTHER

A commentary using Ancient Bible Study Methods

Michael Harvey Koplitz

Acknowledgment

This work could not have been accomplished without Dr. Anne Davis, who taught me Ancient (Hebraic) Bible study methods, and my two study partners, Rev. Dr. Robert Cook, and Pastor Sandra Koplitz. We know that the journey has just started and will last a lifetime. The discovery of the depths of God's Word is waiting for us to find.

Table of Contents

Introduction

While I was attending Seminary earning my M. Div. degree, I started to question what the instructors and reference books were saying about the Scriptures. One of the ideas being offered then was that the Bible was full of errors and not factual. I found that attitude disturbing for Seminary instructors to be teaching. After all, the Seminary experience is to train pastors to go out into God's world and preach the Bible. How can you preach the Bible if you believe what these instructors are teaching? The methods that were being taught to examine the Bible just seemed inaccurate to me.

After graduating from Seminary, I spent much time reading different views about the Bible. I eventually read the Zohar. This collection of Midrashim is considered the secret work of the Torah, according to Kabbalists. Also, I learned quite a bit about Messianic Judaism. Their view of the Bible is quite different from the Seminary view.

I decided that the biblical interpretation that was being taught in Seminary was not the biblical interpretation the people heard when Jesus Christ (whose Hebraic name is Yeshua) preached. I went on a quest to learn what the people of Yeshua's day thought about Scripture, and what they thought when the Scriptures were read. This quest led me to Dr. Anne Davis and The Bible Learning University. Dr. Davis was in search of the same thing I was searching for. She had made many discoveries that helped me in my quest. I earned the Ph. D. degree from The Bible Learning University in Hebraic Studies in Christianity concentrating on ancient Bible Studies methods.

Finally, I found someone who believed that the church had placed almost 1900 years of their theological ideas about the Scriptures and in many places possibly distorting its original meaning. What is also essential to hear is that the basic tenants of Yeshua as God's Messiah, my Lord and Savior are in the Bible. My faith in Yeshua is stronger now that I have learned from Dr. Davis how to study the Scriptures in the same manner that the people did in Yeshua's day.

I have included an article that describes the differences between Greek learning methods and Hebraic learning methods. Please do not skip this chapter unless you are familiar with ancient Bible study methods because if you do, then the analysis and commentary that follows may become difficult for you to understand.

Our God is vast and infinite, and so is His Word. May God bless you in your discovery of what God's Word is about.

The book of Esther starts with conflict. It is the only book that was not included in the Dead Sea Scrolls of the Essene. According to historians the Essene community did not celebrate the minor holiday of Purim. In addition, the book of Esther does not contain the tetragrammaton name of the LORD. This may be a reason for the community's rejection of the book. Modern Judaism celebrates the holiday of Purim with the reading of the scroll in a party mode. The Jews of the Perisan Empire were under the threat of extinction. Through the bravery of Mordaicai and Esther the people were saved. The Purim celebration can be described as 1) They tried to kill us, 2) We won, 3) Let us eat.

"The Talmud bears witness that Esther was accepted as scripture by the Jews in the first two centuries A.D."[1] If Esther was a queen in Persia then the dating of the writing could be done by who the king of Persia was at the time. It is possible that Esther is a

---

[1] Bush, F. W. (1996). *Ruth, Esther* (Vol. 9, p. 274). Dallas: Word, Incorporated.

folktale about a heroine who saved her people. The lessons about being a part of the greater community and a willingness to suffer for the greater community is clear in this writing. When Yeshua lived His main purpose was the community. Esther could be seen as a foreshadowing of what the Messiah Yeshua was going to do. Esther did not try to change anything. However, she was willing to offer her life for her people. Yeshua offered His life for all the people of the world.

The main differences between the Greek method and the Hebraic method of teaching

Once a student becomes aware of these two teaching styles, the student will be able to determine if the class attended or if a book read, whether the teaching method is either a Greek or Hebraic method. In the Greek manner, the instructor is always right because of advanced knowledge. In the college situation, it is because the professor has his/her Ph.D. in some area of study, so one assumes that he or she knows everything about the topic. For example, Rodney Dangerfield played the role of a middle-aged man going to college. His English midterm was to write about Kurt Vonnegut Jr. Since he did not understand any of Vonnegut's books he hired Vonnegut himself to write the midterm. When he received the paper from the English Professor told Dangerfield that whoever wrote the paper knew nothing about Vonnegut. The professor's words are an example of the Greek method of teaching. Did the Ph.D. English professor think that she knew more about Vonnegut's writings than Vonnegut did? [2]

In the Greek teaching method, the professor or the instructor claims to be the authority. If one attends a Bible study class and the class leader says, "I will teach you the only way to understand this biblical book," you may want to consider the implications. This method is standard since most Seminaries and Bible colleges teach a Greek mode of learning, which is the same method the church has been utilizing for centuries.

---

[2] *Back to School.* Performed by Rodney Dangerfield. Hollywood: CA: Paper Clip Productions, 1986. DVD.

Hebraic teaching methods are different. The teacher wants the students to challenge what they hear. It is through questioning that a student can learn. Also, the teacher wants his/her students to excel to a point where the student becomes the teacher.

If two rabbis come together to discuss a passage of Scripture, the result will be at least ten different opinions. All points of view are acceptable if each is supported by biblical evidence. It is permissible and encouraged that students develop many ideas. There is a depth to God's Word, and God wants us to find all His messages contained in the Scripture.

Seeking out the meaning of the Scriptures beyond the literal meaning is essential to understand God's Word fully.[3] The Greek method of learning the Scriptures has prevailed over the centuries. One problem is that only the literal interpretation of Scripture was often viewed as valid, as prompted by Martin Luther's "sola literalis" meaning that just the literal translation of Scripture was accurate. The Fundamentalist movements of today base their beliefs on the literal interpretation of the Scripture. Therefore, they do not believe that God placed more profound, hidden, or secret meanings in the Word.

The students of the Scriptures who learn through Hebraic training and understanding have drawn a different conclusion. The Hebrew language itself leads to different possible interpretations because of the construction of the language. The Hebraic method of Bible study opens avenues of thought about God's revelations in the Scripture never considered. Not all questions about the Scripture studied will have an

---

[3] Davis, Anne Kimball. *The Synoptic Gospels*. MP3. Albuquerque: NM: BibleInteract, 2012.

immediate answer. If so, it becomes the responsibility of the learners to uncover the meaning. Also, remember that many opinions about the meaning of Scripture are also acceptable.

Methodology

The methodology employed is to use First Century Scripture study methods integrated with the customs and culture of Yeshua's day to examine the Hebrew and Christian Scriptures, thus gathering a more in-depth understanding by learning the Scriptures in the way the people of Yeshua's day did.

I have titled the methodology of analyzing a passage of Scripture in a Hebraic manner the "Process of Discovery." The author developed this methodology which brings together the various areas of linguistic and cultural understanding. There are several sections to the process, and not all the parts apply to every passage of Scripture. The overall result of developing this process is to give the reader a framework for studying the word in more depth.

The "Process of Discovery" starts with a Scripture passage. An examination of the linguistic structure of the passage is next. The linguistic structure includes parallelism, chiastic structures, and repetition. Formatting the passage in its linguistic form allows the reader to be able to visualize what the first century CE listener was hearing. Their corresponding sections label the chiasms, for example, A, B, C, B', A.' Not all passages of the Scriptures have a poetic form.

The next step is to "question the narrative." The questioning the narrative process assuming the reader knows nothing about the passage. Therefore, the questions go from the simple to the complex. The next task is to identify any linguistic patterns. Linguistic patterns include, but are not limited to irony, simile, metaphor, symbolism, idioms, hyperbole, figurative language, personification, and allegory.

A review of any translation inconsistencies discovered between the English NAU version and either the Hebrew or Greek versions is done. There are times when a Hebrew or Greek word is translated in more than one way. Inconsistencies also can be created by the translation committee, which may have decided to use traditional language instead of the actual translation. The decision of the translation committee is in the Preface or Introduction to the Bible. Perhaps some of the inconsistencies were intentionally added to convey some deeper meaning. An examination for every discrepancy is done.

The passage is analyzed for any echoes of the Hebrew Scriptures in the Christian Scriptures. Using a passage from the Hebrew Scriptures in the Christian Scriptures, an echo occurs.[4] Also, echoes are found when Torah (Genesis through Deuteronomy) passages , in other Hebrew Bible books. Cross-references in the Scripture are references from one verse to another verse which can assist the reader in understanding the verse.

The names of persons mentioned in the passage are listed. Many of the Hebrew names have meaning and may be associated with places or actions. Jewish parents used to name their children based on what they felt God had in store for their child. An example of this is Abraham whose original name was Abram and was changed to mean eternal father (God changed Abram's name to Abraham indicating a function he was to perform). When the Hebrew Bible gives names, many of the occurrences mean

---

[4] Mitzvot are the 613 commandments found in the Torah that please God. There are positive and negative commandments. The list was first development by Maimonides. The full list can be found at: ttp://www.jewfaq.org/613.htm.

something unique. The same importance can occur for the names of places. The time it takes to travel between locations can supply insight into the event.

Key phrases are identified in verses when they are essential to an understanding of that passage. There are no rules for selecting the keywords. Searching for other occurrences of the keywords in Scripture in a concordance is necessary to understand the word's usage; this must be done in either Hebrew or Greek, not in English. A classic Hebraic approach is to find the usage of a word in the Scripture by finding other verses that contain the word. The usage of a word, in its original language, is discovered by searching the Scripture in the language of the word. Verses that contain the word are identified, and a pattern for the usage of the word discovered. Each verse is examined to see what the usage of the word is which, may reveal a model for the word's usage. For Hebrew words the first usage of the word in the Scripture, primarily if used in the Torah, is essential. For the Greek words, the Christian Scriptures are used to determine the word usage in the Scripture. Sometimes finding the equivalent Greek word in the Septuagint then analyzing its usage in Hebrew can be very helpful.

The Rules of Hillel are used when applicable. Hillel was a Torah scholar who lived shortly before Yeshua's day. Hillel developed several rules for Torah students to interpret the Scriptures which refer to halachic Midrash. In several cases, these rules are helpful in the analysis of the Scripture.

The cultural implications from the period of the writing are done after the linguistic analysis is completed. The culture is crucial because it is not explicitly referenced in the biblical narratives as indicated earlier.

From the linguistic analysis and the cultural understanding, it is possible to obtain a deeper meaning of the Scripture beyond the literal meaning of the plain text. That is what the listeners of Yeshua's time were doing. They put the linguistics and the culture together without even having to contemplate it. They simply did it.

The analysis will lead to a set of findings explaining what the passage meant in Yeshua's day. Most of the time the Hebraic analysis leads to the desire for more in-depth analysis to fully understand what Yeshua was talking about or what was happening to Him. Whatever the result, a new more in-depth understanding of the Scripture is obtained.

The components of the Process of Discovery are:

Language

Process of Discovery

Linguistics Section

Linguistic Structure

Discussion

Questioning the Passage

Verse Comparison of citations or proof text

Translation Inconsistencies

Biblical Personalities

Biblical Locations

Phrase Study

Scripture cross-references

Linguistic Echoes

Only the areas needed for each chapter is included.

Chapter One

Language

New American Standard 1995	Hebrew
[1] Now it took place in the days of Ahasuerus, the Ahasuerus who reigned from India to Ethiopia over 127 provinces, [2] in those days as King Ahasuerus sat on his royal throne which *was* at the citadel in Susa, [3] in the third year of his reign he gave a banquet for all his princes and attendants, the army *officers* of Persia and Media, the nobles and the princes of his provinces being in his presence. [4] And he displayed the riches of his royal glory and the splendor of his great majesty for many days, 180 days. [5] When these days were completed, the king gave a banquet lasting seven days for all the people who were present at the citadel in Susa, from the greatest to the least, in the court of the garden of the king's palace. [6] *There were hangings of* fine white and violet linen held by cords of fine purple linen on silver rings and marble columns, *and* couches of gold and silver on a mosaic pavement of porphyry, marble, mother-of-pearl and precious stones. [7] Drinks were served in golden vessels of various kinds, and the royal wine was plentiful according to the king's bounty.	וַיְהִי בִּימֵי אֲחַשְׁוֵרוֹשׁ הוּא אֲחַשְׁוֵרוֹשׁ הַמֹּלֵךְ מֵהֹדּוּ וְעַד־כּוּשׁ שֶׁבַע וְעֶשְׂרִים וּמֵאָה מְדִינָה:2 בַּיָּמִים הָהֵם כְּשֶׁבֶת הַמֶּלֶךְ אֲחַשְׁוֵרוֹשׁ עַל כִּסֵּא מַלְכוּתוֹ אֲשֶׁר בְּשׁוּשַׁן הַבִּירָה: 3 בִּשְׁנַת שָׁלוֹשׁ לְמָלְכוֹ עָשָׂה מִשְׁתֶּה לְכָל־שָׂרָיו וַעֲבָדָיו חֵילוֹ פָּרַס וּמָדַי הַפַּרְתְּמִים וְשָׂרֵי הַמְּדִינוֹת לְפָנָיו: 4 בְּהַרְאֹתוֹ אֶת־עֹשֶׁר כְּבוֹד מַלְכוּתוֹ וְאֶת־יְקָר תִּפְאֶרֶת גְּדוּלָּתוֹ יָמִים רַבִּים שְׁמוֹנִים וּמְאַת יוֹם: 5 וּבִמְלוֹאת הַיָּמִים הָאֵלֶּה עָשָׂה הַמֶּלֶךְ לְכָל־הָעָם הַנִּמְצְאִים בְּשׁוּשַׁן הַבִּירָה לְמִגָּדוֹל וְעַד־קָטָן מִשְׁתֶּה שִׁבְעַת יָמִים בַּחֲצַר גִּנַּת בִּיתַן הַמֶּלֶךְ: 6 חוּר כַּרְפַּס וּתְכֵלֶת אָחוּז בְּחַבְלֵי־בוּץ וְאַרְגָּמָן עַל־גְּלִילֵי כֶסֶף וְעַמּוּדֵי שֵׁשׁ מִטּוֹת זָהָב וָכֶסֶף עַל רִצְפַת בַּהַט־וָשֵׁשׁ וְדַר וְסֹחָרֶת: 7 וְהַשְׁקוֹת בִּכְלֵי זָהָב וְכֵלִים מִכֵּלִים שׁוֹנִים וְיֵין מַלְכוּת רָב כְּיַד הַמֶּלֶךְ: 8 וְהַשְּׁתִיָּה כַדָּת אֵין אֹנֵס כִּי־כֵן יִסַּד הַמֶּלֶךְ עַל כָּל־רַב בֵּיתוֹ לַעֲשׂוֹת כִּרְצוֹן אִישׁ־וָאִישׁ: 9 גַּם וַשְׁתִּי הַמַּלְכָּה עָשְׂתָה מִשְׁתֵּה נָשִׁים בֵּית הַמַּלְכוּת אֲשֶׁר לַמֶּלֶךְ אֲחַשְׁוֵרוֹשׁ: ס 10 בַּיּוֹם הַשְּׁבִיעִי כְּטוֹב לֵב־הַמֶּלֶךְ בַּיָּיִן אָמַר לִמְהוּמָן בִּזְּתָא חַרְבוֹנָא בִּגְתָא וַאֲבַגְתָא זֵתַר וְכַרְכַּס שִׁבְעַת הַסָּרִיסִים הַמְשָׁרְתִים אֶת־פְּנֵי הַמֶּלֶךְ אֲחַשְׁוֵרוֹשׁ: 11 לְהָבִיא אֶת־וַשְׁתִּי הַמַּלְכָּה לִפְנֵי הַמֶּלֶךְ בְּכֶתֶר מַלְכוּת לְהַרְאוֹת הָעַמִּים וְהַשָּׂרִים אֶת־יָפְיָהּ כִּי־טוֹבַת מַרְאֶה הִיא:

8 The drinking was *done* according to the law, there was no compulsion, for so the king had given orders to each official of his household that he should do according to the desires of each person.

9 Queen Vashti also gave a banquet for the women in the palace which belonged to King Ahasuerus.

10 On the seventh day, when the heart of the king was merry with wine, he commanded Mehuman, Biztha, Harbona, Bigtha, Abagtha, Zethar and Carkas, the seven eunuchs who served in the presence of King Ahasuerus,

11 to bring Queen Vashti before the king with *her* royal crown in order to display her beauty to the people and the princes, for she was beautiful.

12 But Queen Vashti refused to come at the king's command delivered by the eunuchs. Then the king became very angry and his wrath burned within him.

13 Then the king said to the wise men who understood the times-- for it was the custom of the king so *to speak* before all who knew law and justice

14 and were close to him: Carshena, Shethar, Admatha, Tarshish, Meres, Marsena and Memucan, the seven princes of Persia and Media who had access to the king's presence and sat in the first place in the kingdom--

15 "According to law, what is to be done with Queen Vashti, because she did not obey the command of King Ahasuerus *delivered* by the eunuchs?"

16 In the presence of the king and the princes, Memucan said, "Queen Vashti has wronged not only the king but *also* all the princes and all the peoples who are in all the provinces of King Ahasuerus.

12 וַתְּמָאֵ֞ן הַמַּלְכָּ֣ה וַשְׁתִּ֗י לָבוֹא֙ בִּדְבַ֣ר הַמֶּ֔לֶךְ אֲשֶׁ֖ר בְּיַ֣ד הַסָּרִיסִ֑ים וַיִּקְצֹ֤ף הַמֶּ֙לֶךְ֙ מְאֹ֔ד וַחֲמָת֖וֹ בָּעֲרָ֥ה בֽוֹ׃

13 וַיֹּ֣אמֶר הַמֶּ֔לֶךְ לַחֲכָמִ֖ים יֹדְעֵ֣י הָֽעִתִּ֑ים כִּי־כֵן֙ דְּבַ֣ר הַמֶּ֔לֶךְ לִפְנֵ֕י כָּל־יֹדְעֵ֖י דָּ֥ת וָדִֽין׃

14 וְהַקָּרֹ֣ב אֵלָ֗יו כַּרְשְׁנָ֤א שֵׁתָר֙ אַדְמָ֣תָא תַרְשִׁ֔ישׁ מֶ֥רֶס מַרְסְנָ֖א מְמוּכָ֑ן שִׁבְעַ֞ת שָׂרֵ֣י ׀ פָּרַ֣ס וּמָדַ֗י רֹאֵי֙ פְּנֵ֣י הַמֶּ֔לֶךְ הַיֹּשְׁבִ֥ים רִאשֹׁנָ֖ה בַּמַּלְכֽוּת׃

15 כְּדָת֙ מַֽה־לַּעֲשׂ֔וֹת בַּמַּלְכָּ֖ה וַשְׁתִּ֑י עַ֣ל ׀ אֲשֶׁ֣ר לֹֽא־עָשְׂתָ֗ה אֶֽת־מַאֲמַר֙ הַמֶּ֣לֶךְ אֲחַשְׁוֵר֔וֹשׁ בְּיַ֖ד הַסָּרִיסִֽים׃ ס

16 וַיֹּ֣אמֶר מומכן [מְמוּכָ֗ן] לִפְנֵ֤י הַמֶּ֙לֶךְ֙ וְהַשָּׂרִ֔ים לֹ֤א עַל־הַמֶּ֙לֶךְ֙ לְבַדּ֔וֹ עָוְתָ֖ה וַשְׁתִּ֣י הַמַּלְכָּ֑ה כִּ֤י עַל־כָּל־הַשָּׂרִים֙ וְעַל־כָּל־הָ֣עַמִּ֔ים אֲשֶׁ֕ר בְּכָל־מְדִינ֖וֹת הַמֶּ֥לֶךְ אֲחַשְׁוֵרֽוֹשׁ׃

17 כִּֽי־יֵצֵ֤א דְבַר־הַמַּלְכָּה֙ עַל־כָּל־הַנָּשִׁ֔ים לְהַבְז֥וֹת בַּעְלֵיהֶ֖ן בְּעֵינֵיהֶ֑ן בְּאָמְרָ֗ם הַמֶּ֣לֶךְ אֲחַשְׁוֵר֡וֹשׁ אָמַ֞ר לְהָבִ֨יא אֶת־וַשְׁתִּ֧י הַמַּלְכָּ֛ה לְפָנָ֖יו וְלֹא־בָֽאָה׃

18 וְֽהַיּ֨וֹם הַזֶּ֜ה תֹּאמַ֣רְנָה ׀ שָׂר֣וֹת פָּֽרַס־וּמָדַ֗י אֲשֶׁ֤ר שָׁמְעוּ֙ אֶת־דְּבַ֣ר הַמַּלְכָּ֔ה לְכֹ֖ל שָׂרֵ֣י הַמֶּ֑לֶךְ וּכְדַ֖י בִּזָּי֥וֹן וָקָֽצֶף׃

19 אִם־עַל־הַמֶּ֣לֶךְ ט֗וֹב יֵצֵ֤א דְבַר־מַלְכוּת֙ מִלְּפָנָ֔יו וְיִכָּתֵ֛ב בְּדָתֵ֥י פָֽרַס־וּמָדַ֖י וְלֹ֣א יַעֲב֑וֹר אֲשֶׁ֨ר לֹֽא־תָב֜וֹא וַשְׁתִּ֗י לִפְנֵי֙ הַמֶּ֣לֶךְ אֲחַשְׁוֵר֔וֹשׁ וּמַלְכוּתָהּ֙ יִתֵּ֣ן הַמֶּ֔לֶךְ לִרְעוּתָ֖הּ הַטּוֹבָ֥ה מִמֶּֽנָּה׃

20 וְנִשְׁמַע֩ פִּתְגָ֨ם הַמֶּ֤לֶךְ אֲשֶֽׁר־יַעֲשֶׂה֙ בְּכָל־מַלְכוּת֔וֹ כִּ֥י רַבָּ֖ה הִ֑יא וְכָל־הַנָּשִׁ֗ים יִתְּנ֤וּ יְקָר֙ לְבַעְלֵיהֶ֔ן לְמִגָּד֖וֹל וְעַד־קָטָֽן׃

21 וַיִּיטַב֙ הַדָּבָ֔ר בְּעֵינֵ֥י הַמֶּ֖לֶךְ וְהַשָּׂרִ֑ים וַיַּ֥עַשׂ הַמֶּ֖לֶךְ כִּדְבַ֥ר מְמוּכָֽן׃

22 וַיִּשְׁלַ֤ח סְפָרִים֙ אֶל־כָּל־מְדִינ֣וֹת הַמֶּ֔לֶךְ אֶל־מְדִינָ֤ה וּמְדִינָה֙ כִּכְתָבָ֔הּ וְאֶל־עַ֥ם וָעָ֖ם כִּלְשׁוֹנ֑וֹ לִהְי֤וֹת כָּל־אִישׁ֙ שֹׂרֵ֣ר בְּבֵית֔וֹ וּמְדַבֵּ֖ר כִּלְשׁ֥וֹן עַמּֽוֹ׃ פ

[17] "For the queen's conduct will become known to all the women causing them to look with contempt on their husbands by saying, 'King Ahasuerus commanded Queen Vashti to be brought in to his presence, but she did not come.'

[18] "This day the ladies of Persia and Media who have heard of the queen's conduct will speak in *the same way* to all the king's princes, and there will be plenty of contempt and anger.

[19] "If it pleases the king, let a royal edict be issued by him and let it be written in the laws of Persia and Media so that it cannot be repealed, that Vashti may no longer come into the presence of King Ahasuerus, and let the king give her royal position to another who is more worthy than she.

[20] "When the king's edict which he will make is heard throughout all his kingdom, great as it is, then all women will give honor to their husbands, great and small."

[21] *This* word pleased the king and the princes, and the king did as Memucan proposed.

[22] So he sent letters to all the king's provinces, to each province according to its script and to every people according to their language, that every man should be the master in his own house and the one who speaks in the language of his own people.

Process of Discovery

Linguistics Section

Linguistic Structure

A [1] Now it took place in the days of Ahasuerus, the Ahasuerus who reigned from India to Ethiopia over 127 provinces, [2] in those days as King Ahasuerus sat on his royal throne which *was* at the citadel in Susa, [3] in the third year of his reign he gave a banquet for all his princes and attendants, the army *officers* of Persia and Media, the nobles and the princes of his provinces being in his presence.[4] And he displayed the riches of his royal glory and the splendor of his great majesty for many days, 180 days.[5] When these days were completed, the king gave a banquet lasting seven days for all the people who were present at the citadel in Susa, from the greatest to the least, in the court of the garden of the king's palace.[6] *There were hangings of* fine white and violet linen held by cords of fine purple linen on silver rings and marble columns, *and* couches of gold and silver on a mosaic pavement of porphyry, marble, mother-of-pearl and precious stones. [7] Drinks were served in golden vessels of various kinds, and the royal wine was plentiful according to the king's bounty. [8] The drinking was *done* according to the law, there was no compulsion, for so the king had given orders to each official of his household that he should do according to the desires of each person. [9] Queen Vashti also gave a banquet for the women in the palace which belonged to King Ahasuerus.

B [10] On the seventh day, when the heart of the king was merry with wine, he commanded Mehuman, Biztha, Harbona, Bigtha, Abagtha, Zethar and Carkas, the seven eunuchs who served in the presence of King Ahasuerus, [11] to bring Queen Vashti before the king with *her* royal crown in order to display her beauty to the people and the princes, for she was beautiful.

C [12] But Queen Vashti refused to come at the king's command delivered by the eunuchs. Then the king became very angry and his wrath burned within him. [13] Then the king said to the wise men who understood the times-- for it was the custom of the king so *to speak* before all who knew law and justice

B' [14] and were close to him: Carshena, Shethar, Admatha, Tarshish, Meres, Marsena and Memucan, the seven princes of Persia and Media who had access to the king's presence and sat in the first place in the kingdom-- [15] "According to law, what is to be done with Queen Vashti, because she did not obey the command of King Ahasuerus *delivered* by the eunuchs?" [16] In the presence of the king and the princes, Memucan said, "Queen Vashti has wronged not only the king but *also* all the princes and all the peoples who are in all the provinces of King Ahasuerus. [17] "For the queen's conduct will become known to all the women causing them to look with contempt on their husbands by saying, 'King Ahasuerus commanded Queen Vashti to be brought in to his presence, but she did not come.' [18] "This day the ladies of Persia and Media who have heard of the queen's conduct will speak in *the same way* to all the king's princes, and there will be plenty of contempt and anger. [19] "If it pleases the king, let a royal edict be issued by him and let it be written in the laws of Persia and Media so that it cannot be repealed, that Vashti may no longer come into the presence of King Ahasuerus, and let the king give her royal position to another who is more worthy than she. [20] "When the king's edict which he will make is heard throughout all his kingdom, great as it is, then all women will give honor to their husbands, great and small."

A' [21] *This* word pleased the king and the princes, and the king did as Memucan proposed. [22] So he sent letters to all the king's provinces, to each province according to its script and to every people according to their language, that every man should be the master in his own house and the one who speaks in the language of his own people.

Discussion

The introduction to the story of Queen Esther is that the then Queen, Vashti, had to be removed from the throne. There are several ideas found in the Targums that talk about why Vashti was ordered to dance before the princes of the Empire and when she refused why she was executed.

Questioning the Passage[5]

1. Who was Esther?

    Esther was a descendant of Sarah. Sarah lived 127 years. The Targum Rishon says that Esther was destined to marry the King because he ruled over 127 provinces, the same number of years that Sarah lived.[6] Since every Hebrew woman is a descendant of Sarah, it could be said that the King was destined to marry a Hebrew woman. According to the story, Esther was the most beautiful woman in all the land. The LORD insured this.

2. Why was the capital of the kingdom on Susa? (v. 2)

    "Susa was chosen by Darius I (521–485) as the site of the main administrative capital of the Persian empire and the king's winter residence."[7]

3. Why was the party and feast at Susa? (v. 2)

    "The Persian palaces at Persepolis and Susa had large assembly halls (Persian: *apadana*) separate from the royal residence that was used for receiving embassies from throughout the empire. Reliefs were made depicting these assemblies— representatives from different provinces bearing gifts—decorated the walls. These reliefs may be correlated with the Greek descriptions, and together they both show that the royal table was of central significance in the political ideology of Persia. The number of guests could be huge, according to some Greek sources. It was a mark of high status to be seated at the king's table.

---

[5] (The questions and answers offered are for discussion purposes. You may have different questions and answers. Remember all questions are valid and all answers must be defendable from Scripture. This applies to this section and to the Culture Section.)

[6] "The Aramaic Bible, the Two Targums of Esther" The Liturgical Press. 1991

[7] Berlin, A. (2001). *Esther* (p. 7). Philadephia: Jewish Publication Society.

Indeed, the groups of guests mentioned in this verse constitute the elite of Persian society."[8]

4. What is the "royal throne?" (v. 2)

"The phrase is redundant and has been interpreted in several ways. Since there were four Persian capitals—Susa, Ecbatana (Hamadan), Babylon, and Persepolis—the phrase may indicate that the king was now in residence in Susa."[9]

This phrase may be indicating that the king's position as king was not being challenged by anyone inside the kingdom nor any enemy outside of the kingdom. The king was secure in his reign.

5. What is the Kingdom of the king? (v. 3)

The Persian Empire was a combination of Persia and Media. Persia was to the east of the Babylonian Empire while Media was in the northwest. It took both nations to join together to topple the Babylonian Empire. The Persian-Media Empire was from India in the east to Media in the west and to Ethiopia in the south.

6. Is there a significance to it being the third year of the king's reign? (v. 3)

The number three signifies a divine influence. The Targum Rishon says that the LORD decreed that Vashti would die nude because she used her influence to try to stop the rebuilding of the Temple. The third year of Ahasuerus says

---

[8] Berlin, A. (2001). *Esther* (pp. 7–8). Philadephia: Jewish Publication Society.

[9] IBID.

that the LORD's influence over him was at its strongest. It was time to remove Vashti so that the Temple at Jerusalem could be rebuilt.

7. Why did the king display his riches for 180 days? (v. 4)

The Targum Rishon says that the King's riches came from several sources. A large portion of the King's riches was left to him by Cyrus the Mede. Cyrus' wealth came from the capture of the Babylonian Empire. Cyrus dug into the bank of the Euphrates and discovered 680 copper vessels filled with pure gold, sparkling gems, yellow emeralds, and other types of gems. Ahasuerus' glory intensified through the wealth that he had. Thus, his power over his kingdom also grew.[10]

The 180 days party is often compared to the 120 days party of Nebuchadnezzar found in the book of Judith (from the Apocrypha). A Babylonian King would not upstage Ahasuerus. Therefore he extended his party to show his triumph over everything that was Babylonian.

Judith 1:1 ¶ It was the twelfth year of the reign of Nebuchadnezzar, who ruled over the Assyrians in the great city of Nineveh. In those days Arphaxad ruled over the Medes in Ecbatana. **2** He built walls around Ecbatana with hewn stones three cubits thick and six cubits long; he made the walls seventy cubits high and fifty cubits wide. **3** At its gates he raised towers one hundred cubits high and sixty cubits wide at the foundations. **4** He made its gates seventy cubits high and forty cubits wide to allow his armies to march out in force and his infantry to form their ranks. **5** Then King Nebuchadnezzar made war against King Arphaxad in the great plain that is on the borders of Ragau. **6** There rallied to him all the people of the hill country and all those who lived along the Euphrates, the Tigris, and the Hydaspes, and, on the plain, Arioch, king of the Elymeans. Thus, many nations joined the forces of the Chaldeans. **7** ¶ Then Nebuchadnezzar, king of the Assyrians, sent messengers to all who lived in Persia and to all who lived in the west, those who lived in Cilicia and Damascus, Lebanon and Antilebanon, and all who

---

[10] "The Aramaic Bible, the Two Targums of Esther" The Liturgical Press. 1991

lived along the seacoast, **8** and those among the nations of Carmel and Gilead, and Upper Galilee and the great plain of Esdraelon, **9** and all who were in Samaria and its towns, and beyond the Jordan as far as Jerusalem and Bethany and Chelous and Kadesh and the river of Egypt, and Tahpanhes and Raamses and the whole land of Goshen, **10** even beyond Tanis and Memphis, and all who lived in Egypt as far as the borders of Ethiopia. **11** But all who lived in the whole region disregarded the summons of Nebuchadnezzar, king of the Assyrians, and refused to join him in the war; for they were not afraid of him, but regarded him as only one man. So they sent back his messengers empty-handed and in disgrace. **12** ¶ Then Nebuchadnezzar became very angry with this whole region, and swore by his throne and kingdom that he would take revenge on the whole territory of Cilicia and Damascus and Syria, that he would kill with his sword also all the inhabitants of the land of Moab, and the people of Ammon, and all Judea, and every one in Egypt, as far as the coasts of the two seas. **13** ¶ In the seventeenth year he led his forces against King Arphaxad and defeated him in battle, overthrowing the whole army of Arphaxad and all his cavalry and all his chariots. **14** Thus he took possession of his towns and came to Ecbatana, captured its towers, plundered its markets, and turned its glory into disgrace. **15** He captured Arphaxad in the mountains of Ragau and struck him down with his spears, thus destroying him once and for all. **16** Then he returned to Nineveh, he and all his combined forces, a vast body of troops; and there he and his forces rested and feasted for one hundred twenty days.

8. What is the significance of a banquet that lasted seven days? (v. 5)

"After the first banquet there was a shorter one, lasting a week, for the residents of the royal city. Excavations at Susa have confirmed that there was a lightly populated residential area in the royal city. The Rabbis take pains to note that only Jews disloyal to their tradition attended this banquet (where nonkosher food and wine were served) and that Mordecai and his associates were not among them."[11]

---

[11] Berlin, A. (2001). *Esther* (p. 8). Philadephia: Jewish Publication Society.

9. What is the significance of the items listed in verse six?

The party for the ordinary people was not held in the King's banquet room. It was held in a location that was accessible to the people of Susa. The Persian Empire was known for its beautiful gardens and tapestries. The court in which the banquet for the people was held is described in verse six.

10. What is royal wine? (v. 7)

Royal wine refers to the best-made wine in the Empire

11. What was the law about drinking? (v. 8)

The Targum Rishon says that each King established the law about drinking. Therefore, the law about drinking at this party was following what Ahasuerus decreed.[12]

At wedding feasts and banquets, the male guests were expected to get intoxicated. It was a sign of honor to the bride and groom. The King decided that this custom was to be avoided at his banquet. Therefore, he created a law that allowed the male guests not to get intoxicated.[13]

12. Who were the women that belonged to the king? (v. 9)

The King owned wealth in treasures and people. The women that Vashti brought together were servants or slaves of the King and would be considered a part of the King's property. Since the King was showing off his wealth, Vashti wanted the princes to see everything the King owned.

---

[12] "The Aramaic Bible, the Two Targums of Esther" The Liturgical Press. 1991

[13] Rocco A. Errico and George M. Lamsa, *Aramaic Light on Ezra through the Song of Solomon* (Smyrna, GA: Noohra Foundation, 2010).

13. Why did Queen Vashti give a banquet for the women in the palace which belonged to King Ahasuerus? (v. 9)

Vashti wanted to assist the King, who was showing off his wealth. She brought the women of the palace together, which the King owned, to show them off. The "palace" of the King was his bedroom, according to the Targum Rishon and Sheni. There is no reason given for Vashti doing this.

14. Is there a significance to there being seven eunuchs? (v. 10)

The Targum Sheni says that the seven eunuchs referenced in verse ten are angels from the LORD who were sent to confuse King Ahasuerus. The number seven refers to the completeness of the LORD. Therefore, the reader can assume that divine intervention was going to take place.

15. What does it mean for the Queen to display her beauty to the people and the princes? (v. 11)

The Targum Rishon says that the LORD decreed that Vashti be executed for her opposition to the rebuilding of the Temple in Jerusalem. Why would the LORD demand this? The Targum Rishon says that Vashti forced Israeli girls to work in the nude and made them beat wool and flax on the Sabbath day, therefore it was decreed upon her to be brought out to the King in the nude and eventually executed in the nude. She was told to bring her royal jewels only. The crown of the Queen was on her head because of the merit of her grandfather, Nebuchadnezzar, who dressed Daniel in purple. Purple was the color of royalty. The crown showed all the people that she was the queen. Thus her true beauty would be shown to the princes because she was good-looking. This would also show the princes another part of the King's wealth. The

LORD honored her royalty but punished her in accordance with the way she treated the Israelite women in her care.[14]

16. What is the first place in the palace? (v. 14)

This verse indicates that the seven princes listed were the closest advisors to King Ahasuerus.

17. Why did the princes believe that Vashti's disobedience would effect the women of the kingdom? (v. 17)

The princes were concerned that a decree of the King was not being obeyed. If the King did not do something about it, then the ordinary citizens of the Empire could also disobey the King's orders without suffering any consequences.

18. Why would the king's edict force women to honor their husbands? (v. 20)

Armed soldiers enforced the laws of the kingdom. The punishment for disobeying a directive of the King was death. Indeed, the wives of the men of the kingdom would have preferred to obey rather than to die.

It was a time of polygamy. Men were afraid to give their wives freedom, and they forced women to obey their husbands no matter what the circumstances. The princes were afraid that if the word spread that Vashti did not immediately

---

[14] IBID.

obey her husband that this idea would spread in the land thus allowing women independence.[15]

Biblical Personalities

1. Vashti (v. 9) – queen of King Ahasuerus (Xerxes in Greek). She was the daughter of the "Evil-Merodakh" son of Nebuchadnezzar (King of Babylon, who Exiled the Hebrew people). Vashti did whatever she could to prevent the rebuilding of the LORD's Temple in Jerusalem. She influenced Ahasuerus to stop the reconstruction of the Temple. For this sin, the Targum Rishon says that the LORD decreed that she be executed in the nude.[16]

King Ahasuerus married into the royal line of Babylon. He may have done this to convince the old guard of the Babylonian Empire that their empire had "evolved" into a new empire. The old royal line was integrated into the new royal line.

The first chapter of the book of Esther tells the story of the LORD's influence on the King that resulted in Vashti's nude execution. The King ordered Vashti to come before his drunken guests to show off her beauty with her royal jewels. That means she was to appear nude, only wearing her royal jewels. When Vashti refused, the princes who were at the feast with the King insisted that she be executed for her disobedience. The King complied, thus fulfilling the decree of the LORD that Vashti was to be executed in the nude.

---

[15] IBID.
[16] "The Aramaic Bible, the Two Targums of Esther" The Liturgical Press. 1991

2. The King – "Ahasuerus was the King of Persia who, according to the Book of Esther ruled from India to Ethiopia. He is believed by 19th-century commentators to be Xerxes I of Persia. Achashverosh, as his name transliterates from Hebrew, was also mentioned in the books of Ezra, Daniel, and Tobit. The most famous appearance of Ahasuerus was as a character in the Book of Esther, in which he searches for a new queen after the death of his wife Vashti and is nearly tricked by his advisor Haman into allowing the Jewish people to be destroyed. He ends up marrying a Jewess, Esther, and appoints her uncle, Mordecai, as his counselor. Together they ruin Haman's plans and save the Jewish people."[17]

3. The names of the seven eunuchs

   The Targum Rishon calls the seven eunuchs angels that the LORD sent to the King.[18]

   a. Mehuman was appointed over trouble

   b. Biztha was to bring shame to the king's house

   c. Harbona was to destroy the house

   d. Bigtha and Abagtha were to squeeze the king, as the Master of the Univese wwas going to squeeze the king like grapes in a wine press.

   e. Zethar and Carcas's purpose was not identified

4. The seven princes as identified in the Targum Sheni are:[19]

   a. Carshena was from Africa

   b. Shethar was from Hindaqi

---

[17] Ahasuerus, accessed November 5, 2019, https://www.jewishvirtuallibrary.org/ahasuerus.
[18] IBID.
[19] IBID.

    c. Admatha was from Edom

    d. Tarshish was from Egypt

    e. Meres was from Meres

    f. Memukhan was from Jerusalem

These seven princes were to personally attend to the needs of the King.

Biblical Locations

1. Susa – "Susa was one of the oldest cities in the world and part of the site is still inhabited as Shush, Khuzestan Province, Iran. Excavations have uncovered evidence of continual habitation dating back to 4200 BCE but that early community grew from an even older one dating back to c. 7000 BCE. Susa was a principal city of the Elamite, Achaemenid Persian, and Parthian empires and was originally known to the Elamites as 'Susan' or 'Susun'. The Greek name for the city was Sousa and the Hebrew, Shushan. It is mentioned in the Bible in the books of Daniel, Ezra, Nehemiah, and most notably the Book of Esther and was said to be the home of both Nehemiah and Daniel."[20]

Culture

Discussion

In Persia, during Esther's time, the fame and glory of the King were manifested by the extravagant palaces and items of gold and silver the King possessed. The King's wealth also included rugs, carpets, and couches.[21]

---

[20] Joshua J. Mark, "Susa," Ancient History Encyclopedia (Ancient History Encyclopedia, November 2, 2019), https://www.ancient.eu/susa/.

[21] Rocco A. Errico and George M. Lamsa, *Aramaic Light on Ezra through the Song of Solomon* (Smyma, GA: Noohra Foundation, 2010).

Eunuchs were employed by the King to attend to his harem. This practice continued in the Middle East until the twentieth century. The name *Mehuman* means "a trustworthy person, a faithful one." The English translations viewed this word as a name. Therefore, there are seven eunuchs listed, which correspond to the seventh day. If *menuman* is translated correctly then there are six eunuchs listed.[22]

No stranger to a Middle Eastern woman of nobility was permitted to see her face. Women covered their faces in the Middle East, going back to time immemorial. When Vashti was ordered to appear naked before the King and his princes, she decided to make a bold statement for all women in the Empire. She did not lower herself to act as an entertainer. In her time, women were considered inferior to men. By standing up to the King, she took the stand that women were not inferior to men and deserved equal respect and dignity.[23]

The generally accepted idea of this chapter is that Vashti was ordered to dance naked before the King and his princes. Taking the culture into account, she was not ordered to dance naked. Instead, she was asked to dance like a belly dancer. She was to remove the veil from her face and allow the princes to see her beautiful face. She refused to lower herself in that manner.

Midrash

Esther Rabbah says that the wise men in verse thirteen were descendants of the tribe of Issachar. This Midrash is based on 1 Chronicles 12:32.

---

[22] IBID.

[23] IBID.

1Chr. 12:32 Of the sons of Issachar, *ª*men who understood the times, with knowledge of what Israel should do, their chiefs *were* two hundred; and all their kinsmen *were* at their command.

Additional Notes from the Targum Rishon

1. Verse five in this Targum says that the uncircumcised men of Israel were at the seven-day drinking party except for Mordecai. The Babylonian Empire had incorporated the brilliant men of Israel into government service. The Persian Empire maintained these Israelites in their positions. Mordecai, Esther's uncle, was one of the Israelite elite and a government official. He remained faithful to the LORD because he did not go to the drinking party nor engaged in any drunkenness.

   The Law of the King was for government officials to engage in the drinking party held by the King. However, no one was compelled to engage. Mordechai did not jeopardize his government position by restaining from the party.

2. Verse seven is referring to the golden vessels that belonged to the LORD's Temple in Jerusalem, which Nebuchadnezzar took when he captured the city and destroyed the LORD's Temple. The Targum says that the other gold vessels that were in the storage room with the vessels from the Temple had the appearance of lead and were unusable. So, the servants brought the Temple's vessels to the King.

Thoughts

The author of Esther ensured that readers would discover that the LORD planned to have King Ahasuerus marry a Jewish woman, and that was Esther (Hadassah). A lesson in the chapter is that if one tortures the LORD's chosen people that one day, the LORD will bring a calamity against the offender. Having the girls work in the nude would have been a torture to them because of the many customs of the Hebrew people in Babylon. The chapter is filled with Semitic storytelling and elaboration sprinkled with theological symbolism and phrases. The chapter introduces the reader to the Persian Empire period and why the King was looking for a new queen. Another lesson is that one must respect the Laws of the LORD. By following the Laws of the LORD, one shows reverence to the LORD.

Interestingly, the Targum Rishon refers to the wise men as descendants of the tribe of Issachar. It is generally believed that all of the Northern Kingdom of Israel's tribes were destroyed when the Assyrians spread them out in their Empire. A remnant of the people did survive.

Chapter Two

Language

New American Standard 1995	Hebrew
[1] After these things when the anger of King Ahasuerus had subsided, he remembered Vashti and what she had done and what had been decreed against her.	אַחַר֙ הַדְּבָרִ֣ים הָאֵ֔לֶּה כְּשֹׁ֕ךְ חֲמַ֖ת הַמֶּ֣לֶךְ אֲחַשְׁוֵר֑וֹשׁ זָכַ֣ר אֶת־וַשְׁתִּ֗י וְאֵ֤ת אֲשֶׁר־עָשָׂ֙תָה֙ וְאֵ֥ת אֲשֶׁר־נִגְזַ֖ר עָלֶֽיהָ׃
[2] Then the king's attendants, who served him, said, "Let beautiful young virgins be sought for the king.	וַיֹּאמְר֥וּ נַעֲרֵֽי־הַמֶּ֖לֶךְ מְשָׁרְתָ֑יו יְבַקְשׁ֥וּ לַמֶּ֛לֶךְ נְעָר֥וֹת בְּתוּל֖וֹת טוֹב֥וֹת מַרְאֶֽה׃
[3] "Let the king appoint overseers in all the provinces of his kingdom that they may gather every beautiful young virgin to the citadel of Susa, to the harem, into the custody of Hegai, the king's eunuch, who is in charge of the women; and let their cosmetics be given *them*.	וְיַפְקֵ֨ד הַמֶּ֣לֶךְ פְּקִידִים֮ בְּכָל־מְדִינ֣וֹת מַלְכוּתוֹ֒ וְיִקְבְּצ֣וּ אֶת־כָּל־נַעֲרָֽה־בְ֠תוּלָה טוֹבַ֨ת מַרְאֶ֜ה אֶל־שׁוּשַׁ֤ן הַבִּירָה֙ אֶל־בֵּ֣ית הַנָּשִׁ֔ים אֶל־יַ֥ד הֵגֶ֛א סְרִ֥יס הַמֶּ֖לֶךְ שֹׁמֵ֣ר הַנָּשִׁ֑ים וְנָת֖וֹן תַּמְרוּקֵיהֶֽן׃
[4] "Then let the young lady who pleases the king be queen in place of Vashti." And the matter pleased the king, and he did accordingly.	וְהַֽנַּעֲרָ֗ה אֲשֶׁ֤ר תִּיטַב֙ בְּעֵינֵ֣י הַמֶּ֔לֶךְ תִּמְלֹ֖ךְ תַּ֣חַת וַשְׁתִּ֑י וַיִּיטַ֧ב הַדָּבָ֛ר בְּעֵינֵ֥י הַמֶּ֖לֶךְ וַיַּ֥עַשׂ כֵּֽן׃ ס
[5] *Now* there was at the citadel in Susa a Jew whose name was Mordecai, the son of Jair, the son of Shimei, the son of Kish, a Benjamite,	אִ֣ישׁ יְהוּדִ֔י הָיָ֖ה בְּשׁוּשַׁ֣ן הַבִּירָ֑ה וּשְׁמ֣וֹ מָרְדֳּכַ֗י בֶּ֣ן יָאִ֧יר בֶּן־שִׁמְעִ֛י בֶּן־קִ֖ישׁ אִ֥ישׁ יְמִינִֽי׃
[6] who had been taken into exile from Jerusalem with the captives who had been exiled with Jeconiah king of Judah, whom Nebuchadnezzar the king of Babylon had exiled.	אֲשֶׁ֤ר הָגְלָה֙ מִיר֣וּשָׁלַ֔יִם עִם־הַגֹּלָה֙ אֲשֶׁ֣ר הָגְלְתָ֔ה עִ֖ם יְכָנְיָ֣ה מֶֽלֶךְ־יְהוּדָ֑ה אֲשֶׁ֣ר הֶגְלָ֔ה נְבוּכַדְנֶאצַּ֖ר מֶ֥לֶךְ בָּבֶֽל׃
[7] He was bringing up Hadassah, that is Esther, his uncle's daughter, for she had no father or mother. Now the young lady was beautiful of form and face, and when	וַיְהִ֨י אֹמֵ֜ן אֶת־הֲדַסָּ֗ה הִ֤יא אֶסְתֵּר֙ בַּת־דֹּד֔וֹ כִּ֛י אֵ֥ין לָ֖הּ אָ֣ב וָאֵ֑ם וְהַנַּעֲרָ֤ה יְפַת־תֹּ֙אַר֙ וְטוֹבַ֣ת מַרְאֶ֔ה וּבְמ֤וֹת אָבִ֙יהָ֙ וְאִמָּ֔הּ לְקָחָ֧הּ מָרְדֳּכַ֛י ל֖וֹ לְבַֽת׃
	[8] וַיְהִ֗י בְּהִשָּׁמַ֤ע דְּבַר־הַמֶּ֙לֶךְ֙ וְדָת֔וֹ וּֽבְהִקָּבֵ֞ץ נְעָר֥וֹת רַבּ֛וֹת אֶל־שׁוּשַׁ֥ן הַבִּירָ֖ה אֶל־יַ֣ד הֵגָ֑י וַתִּלָּקַ֤ח אֶסְתֵּר֙ אֶל־בֵּ֣ית הַמֶּ֔לֶךְ אֶל־יַ֥ד הֵגַ֖י שֹׁמֵ֥ר הַנָּשִֽׁים׃
	[9] וַתִּיטַ֨ב הַנַּעֲרָ֣ה בְעֵינָיו֮ וַתִּשָּׂ֣א חֶ֣סֶד לְפָנָיו֒ וַ֠יְבַהֵל אֶת־תַּמְרוּקֶ֤יהָ וְאֶת־מָנוֹתֶ֙הָ֙ לָתֵ֣ת לָ֔הּ וְאֵת֙ שֶׁ֣בַע הַנְּעָר֔וֹת הָרְאֻי֥וֹת לָֽתֶת־לָ֖הּ מִבֵּ֣ית הַמֶּ֑לֶךְ וַיְשַׁנֶּ֧הָ וְאֶת־נַעֲרוֹתֶ֛יהָ לְט֖וֹב בֵּ֥ית הַנָּשִֽׁים׃

her father and her mother died, Mordecai took her as his own daughter.

8 So it came about when the command and decree of the king were heard and many young ladies were gathered to the citadel of Susa into the custody of Hegai, that Esther was taken to the king's palace into the custody of Hegai, who was in charge of the women.

9 Now the young lady pleased him and found favor with him. So he quickly provided her with her cosmetics and food, gave her seven choice maids from the king's palace and transferred her and her maids to the best place in the harem.

10 Esther did not make known her people or her kindred, for Mordecai had instructed her that she should not make *them* known.

11 Every day Mordecai walked back and forth in front of the court of the harem to learn how Esther was and how she fared.

12 Now when the turn of each young lady came to go in to King Ahasuerus, after the end of her twelve months under the regulations for the women-- for the days of their beautification were completed as follows: six months with oil of myrrh and six months with spices and the cosmetics for women--

13 the young lady would go in to the king in this way: anything that she desired was given her to take with her from the harem to the king's palace.

14 In the evening she would go in and in the morning she would return to the second harem, to the custody of Shaashgaz, the king's eunuch who was in charge of the concubines. She would not again go in to the king unless the king

10 לֹא־הִגִּידָה אֶסְתֵּר אֶת־עַמָּהּ וְאֶת־מוֹלַדְתָּהּ כִּי מָרְדֳּכַי צִוָּה עָלֶיהָ אֲשֶׁר לֹא־תַגִּיד:

11 וּבְכָל־יוֹם וָיוֹם מָרְדֳּכַי מִתְהַלֵּךְ לִפְנֵי חֲצַר בֵּית־הַנָּשִׁים לָדַעַת אֶת־שְׁלוֹם אֶסְתֵּר וּמַה־יֵּעָשֶׂה בָּהּ:

12 וּבְהַגִּיעַ תֹּר נַעֲרָה וְנַעֲרָה לָבוֹא אֶל־הַמֶּלֶךְ אֲחַשְׁוֵרוֹשׁ מִקֵּץ הֱיוֹת לָהּ כְּדָת הַנָּשִׁים שְׁנֵים עָשָׂר חֹדֶשׁ כִּי כֵּן יִמְלְאוּ יְמֵי מְרוּקֵיהֶן שִׁשָּׁה חֳדָשִׁים בְּשֶׁמֶן הַמֹּר וְשִׁשָּׁה חֳדָשִׁים בַּבְּשָׂמִים וּבְתַמְרוּקֵי הַנָּשִׁים:

13 וּבָזֶה הַנַּעֲרָה בָּאָה אֶל־הַמֶּלֶךְ אֵת כָּל־אֲשֶׁר תֹּאמַר יִנָּתֵן לָהּ לָבוֹא עִמָּהּ מִבֵּית הַנָּשִׁים עַד־בֵּית הַמֶּלֶךְ:

14 בָּעֶרֶב הִיא בָאָה וּבַבֹּקֶר הִיא שָׁבָה אֶל־בֵּית הַנָּשִׁים שֵׁנִי אֶל־יַד שַׁעֲשְׁגַז סְרִיס הַמֶּלֶךְ שֹׁמֵר הַפִּילַגְשִׁים לֹא־תָבוֹא עוֹד אֶל־הַמֶּלֶךְ כִּי אִם־חָפֵץ בָּהּ הַמֶּלֶךְ וְנִקְרְאָה בְשֵׁם:

15 וּבְהַגִּיעַ תֹּר־אֶסְתֵּר בַּת־אֲבִיחַיִל דֹּד מָרְדֳּכַי אֲשֶׁר לָקַח־לוֹ לְבַת לָבוֹא אֶל־הַמֶּלֶךְ לֹא בִקְשָׁה דָּבָר כִּי אִם אֶת־אֲשֶׁר יֹאמַר הֵגַי סְרִיס־הַמֶּלֶךְ שֹׁמֵר הַנָּשִׁים וַתְּהִי אֶסְתֵּר נֹשֵׂאת חֵן בְּעֵינֵי כָּל־רֹאֶיהָ:

16 וַתִּלָּקַח אֶסְתֵּר אֶל־הַמֶּלֶךְ אֲחַשְׁוֵרוֹשׁ אֶל־בֵּית מַלְכוּתוֹ בַּחֹדֶשׁ הָעֲשִׂירִי הוּא־חֹדֶשׁ טֵבֵת בִּשְׁנַת־שֶׁבַע לְמַלְכוּתוֹ:

17 וַיֶּאֱהַב הַמֶּלֶךְ אֶת־אֶסְתֵּר מִכָּל־הַנָּשִׁים וַתִּשָּׂא־חֵן וָחֶסֶד לְפָנָיו מִכָּל־הַבְּתוּלֹת וַיָּשֶׂם כֶּתֶר־מַלְכוּת בְּרֹאשָׁהּ וַיַּמְלִיכֶהָ תַּחַת וַשְׁתִּי:

18 וַיַּעַשׂ הַמֶּלֶךְ מִשְׁתֶּה גָדוֹל לְכָל־שָׂרָיו וַעֲבָדָיו אֵת מִשְׁתֵּה אֶסְתֵּר וַהֲנָחָה לַמְּדִינוֹת עָשָׂה וַיִּתֵּן מַשְׂאֵת כְּיַד הַמֶּלֶךְ:

19 וּבְהִקָּבֵץ בְּתוּלוֹת שֵׁנִית וּמָרְדֳּכַי יֹשֵׁב בְּשַׁעַר־הַמֶּלֶךְ:

20 אֵין אֶסְתֵּר מַגֶּדֶת מוֹלַדְתָּהּ וְאֶת־עַמָּהּ כַּאֲשֶׁר צִוָּה עָלֶיהָ מָרְדֳּכַי וְאֶת־מַאֲמַר מָרְדֳּכַי אֶסְתֵּר עֹשָׂה כַּאֲשֶׁר הָיְתָה בְאָמְנָה אִתּוֹ: ס

delighted in her and she was summoned by name.

¹⁵ Now when the turn of Esther, the daughter of Abihail the uncle of Mordecai who had taken her as his daughter, came to go in to the king, she did not request anything except what Hegai, the king's eunuch who was in charge of the women, advised. And Esther found favor in the eyes of all who saw her.

¹⁶ So Esther was taken to King Ahasuerus to his royal palace in the tenth month which is the month Tebeth, in the seventh year of his reign.

¹⁷ The king loved Esther more than all the women, and she found favor and kindness with him more than all the virgins, so that he set the royal crown on her head and made her queen instead of Vashti.

¹⁸ Then the king gave a great banquet, Esther's banquet, for all his princes and his servants; he also made a holiday for the provinces and gave gifts according to the king's bounty.

¹⁹ When the virgins were gathered together the second time, then Mordecai was sitting at the king's gate.

²⁰ Esther had not yet made known her kindred or her people, even as Mordecai had commanded her; for Esther did what Mordecai told her as she had done when under his care.

²¹ In those days, while Mordecai was sitting at the king's gate, Bigthan and Teresh, two of the king's officials from those who guarded the door, became angry and sought to lay hands on King Ahasuerus.

²² But the plot became known to Mordecai and he told Queen Esther, and

בַּיָּמִים הָהֵם וּמָרְדֳּכַי יוֹשֵׁב בְּשַׁעַר־הַמֶּלֶךְ ²¹ קָצַף בִּגְתָן וָתֶרֶשׁ שְׁנֵי־סָרִיסֵי הַמֶּלֶךְ מִשֹּׁמְרֵי הַסַּף וַיְבַקְשׁוּ לִשְׁלֹחַ יָד בַּמֶּלֶךְ אֲחַשְׁוֵרֹשׁ׃ וַיִּוָּדַע הַדָּבָר לְמָרְדֳּכַי וַיַּגֵּד לְאֶסְתֵּר ²² הַמַּלְכָּה וַתֹּאמֶר אֶסְתֵּר לַמֶּלֶךְ בְּשֵׁם מָרְדֳּכָי׃ וַיְבֻקַּשׁ הַדָּבָר וַיִּמָּצֵא וַיִּתָּלוּ שְׁנֵיהֶם עַל־עֵץ ²³ וַיִּכָּתֵב בְּסֵפֶר דִּבְרֵי הַיָּמִים לִפְנֵי הַמֶּלֶךְ׃ פ

(Est. 2:1-23 WTT)

Esther informed the king in Mordecai's name.
²³ Now when the plot was investigated and found *to be so,* they were both hanged on a gallows; and it was written in the Book of the Chronicles in the king's presence.

Process of Discovery

Linguistics Section

Linguistic Structure

A [1] After these things when the anger of King Ahasuerus had subsided, he remembered Vashti and what she had done and what had been decreed against her. [2] Then the king's attendants, who served him, said, "Let beautiful young virgins be sought for the king. [3] "Let the king appoint overseers in all the provinces of his kingdom that they may gather every beautiful young virgin to the citadel of Susa, to the harem, into the custody of Hegai, the king's eunuch, who is in charge of the women; and let their cosmetics be given *them.* [4] "Then let the young lady who pleases the king be queen in place of Vashti." And the matter pleased the king, and he did accordingly.

B [5] *Now* there was at the citadel in Susa a Jew whose name was Mordecai, the son of Jair, the son of Shimei, the son of Kish, a Benjamite, [6] who had been taken into exile from Jerusalem with the captives who had been exiled with Jeconiah king of Judah, whom Nebuchadnezzar the king of Babylon had exiled. [7] He was bringing up Hadassah, that is Esther, his uncle's daughter, for she had no father or mother. Now the young lady was beautiful of form and face, and when her father and her mother died, Mordecai took her as his own daughter.

C [8] So it came about when the command and decree of the king were heard and many young ladies were gathered to the citadel of Susa into the custody of Hegai, that Esther was taken to the king's palace into the custody of Hegai, who was in charge of the women. [9] Now the young lady pleased him and found favor with him. So he quickly provided her with her cosmetics and food, gave her seven choice maids from the king's palace and transferred her and her maids to the best place in the harem. [10] Esther did not make known her people or her kindred, for Mordecai had instructed her that she should not make *them* known.

D [11] Every day Mordecai walked back and forth in front of the court of the harem to learn how Esther was and how she fared.

C' [12] Now when the turn of each young lady came to go in to King Ahasuerus, after the end of her twelve months under the regulations for the women-- for the days of their beautification were completed as follows: six months with oil of myrrh and six months with spices and the cosmetics for women-- [13] the young lady would go in to the king in this way: anything that she desired was given her to take with her from the harem to the king's palace. [14] In the evening she would go in and in the morning she would return to the second harem, to the custody of Shaashgaz, the king's eunuch who was in charge of the concubines. She would not again go in to the king unless the king delighted in her and she was summoned by name.

B' [15] Now when the turn of Esther, the daughter of Abihail the uncle of Mordecai who had taken her as his daughter, came to go in to the king, she did not request anything except what Hegai, the king's eunuch who was in charge of the women, advised. And Esther found favor in the eyes of all who saw her. [16] So Esther was taken to King Ahasuerus to his royal palace in the tenth month which is the month Tebeth, in the seventh year of his reign.

A' [17] The king loved Esther more than all the women, and she found favor and kindness with him more than all the virgins, so that he set the royal crown on her head and made her queen instead of Vashti. [18] Then the king gave a great banquet, Esther's banquet, for all his princes and his servants; he also made a holiday for the provinces and gave gifts according to the king's bounty.

A [19] When the virgins were gathered together the second time, then Mordecai was sitting at the king's gate.

B [20] Esther had not yet made known her kindred or her people, even as Mordecai had commanded her; for Esther did what Mordecai told her as she had done when under his care.
A' [21] In those days, while Mordecai was sitting at the king's gate, Bigthan and Teresh, two of the king's officials from those who guarded the door, became angry and sought to lay hands on King Ahasuerus.

B' [22] But the plot became known to Mordecai and he told Queen Esther, and Esther informed the king in Mordecai's name. [23] Now when the plot was investigated and found *to be so*, they were both hanged on a gallows; and it was written in the Book of the Chronicles in the king's presence.

Discussion

This chapter consists of two chiasms. The first chiasm is how Esther was selected by King Ahasuerus to become the Queen of the Persian Empire after Vashti was removed. The second chiasm is the plot to kill the King, which Mordecai discovered. He conveyed the information to Esther, who told the King.

Questioning the Passage

1. What does it mean that the King remembered Vashti? (v. 1)

    The Targum Rishon said when King Ahasuerus sobered up from his wine feast, he asked what happened to Queen Vashti. The seven princes told the King that the King had pronounced a death sentence on the Queen because she refused to come before him nude. The King told the princes that he did not order Vashti to be executed. Instead, the King wanted her removed from the office of Queen. King Ahasuerus became extremely angry at the princes, and they were hung together on seven gallows.[24]

    The Targum Sheni says that King Ahasuerus was not angry at Vashti because he was drunk at the time when the princes talked him into the decree for Vashti's death. Therefore, the King decreed that the seven princes were to be removed from the kingdom. The Targum also says that because Nebuchadnezzar killed the sages of Judea that his family line was to come to an end. When Vashti was killed, Nebuchadnezzar's family line came to an end.[25]

---

[24] "The Aramaic Bible, the Two Targums of Esther" The Liturgical Press. 1991
[25] IBID.

2. What does it mean to please the King? (v. 4)

   The answer to this question is found later in the chapter. Each virgin would go to see the King in the evening. The next morning they would leave the King and become a part of the second harem of the King, who were the concubines. Therefore, "pleasing" the King has to mean to please him sexually.

3. Why is it important to know that Mordecai was from the tribe of Benjamin and what his heritage was? (v. 5)

   The phrase "a Jewish man," which precedes the introduction of Mordicai, indicates that he is from the tribe of Judah, refer to the Phrase study. However, Modecai was not from Judah but rather from the tribe of Benjamin. The author felt it necessary to distinguish Mordicai's true heritage. The Targum Sheni traces his ancestry back to Benjamin.

   The Targum Rishon says that Mordecai was comparable to myrrh. The Targum Rishon indicates that the name Mordecai comes from the same root word as myrrh. Mordecai was a pious man demonstrating piety for the Jewish people daily.[26]

   The ancestry is essential because Shimei, the son of Kish, insulted King David and whom Joab wanted to kill. However, David did not let him do it because David consulted the spirit of prophecy and foresaw that Mordecai and Esther the redeemers would descend from him. Shimei was killed after he stopped procreating. This note is found in Targum Rishon and Targum Sheni.[27]

---

[26] IBID.

[27] IBID.

4. What is the purpose of the short history lesson in verse six?

    The history is vital because Mordecai was a part of the Jewish community that lived in the capital of the Babylonian Empire. When the Persians took control of the entire community, Daniel moved to the citadel at Susa along with a large number of Hebrews.[28]

5. Why did Esther have two names? (v. 7)

    Hadassah was her Hebrew name. Esther was the name she used when in the presence of Gentiles. Dual naming was, and still is, a common practice with Hebrew people.

6. Why was it necessary to repeat that Hegai was in charge of the virgins? (v. 8)

    The mention of the name Hegai twice is because when the King sought to gather all the virgins together, Mordecai hid Esther. The guards of the King came to Mordecai, but they could not find Esther. The King then issued a decree that any virgins hiding from the king's guards, and those assisting were to be executed. Mordecai panicked and brought Esther out for the guards to take to the palace. This explanation is from the Targum Sheni.[29]

7. Why is Esther referred to as a young woman in verse nine?

    This verse indicates that when Esther arrived at the palace, Hegai was fond of her. He gave her the best of the cosmetics available for her beautification. The Targum Rishon says that she was also given royal garments and jewelry. Esther

---

[28] IBID.
[29] IBID.

was also given seven maidens who attended to her every need. The seven maidens each had a specific day of the week to attend to Esther.

Yeshulta – the first day of the week

Ruq'a – the second day of the week

Genonitha – the third day of the week

Nehoritha – the fourth day of the week

Ruhashitha – the fifth day of the week

Hurfitha – the sixth day of the week

Regoitha – the Shabbat day of the week

The Targum Sheni says that Esther received the seven maidens but did not name them. The Targum Sheni says that Esther gave the king's wine, which was given to her, to the seven maidens.[30]

8. Why did Mordecai tell Esther not to reveal her heritage? (v. 10)

   According to the Targum Sheni, Mordecai was concerned that if Esther revealed her heritage that the King would have her put to death. Mordecai believed that if the King would kill Vashti because she would not come before him nude, then the King could kill Esther for being a Hebrew.

---

[30] IBID.

9. What is the twelve-month regulation? (v. 12)

There is no indication in the Scripture or in historical records as to why the beautification period was twelve months.

"Scented oils and ointments were used by this time to clean and soften the skin and mask the body odor. Dyes and natural paint was used to color the face, mainly for ceremonial and religious occasions. Rich people applied minerals to their faces, skin (Iranians use roshoor), and used oiled-based perfumes in their bath. Aromatherapy was used extensively by all the major civilizations of the time including Chinese. An ancient Chinese medical book dated around 2,700 BC contains cures involving over three hundred different aromatic herbs. Traditional Indian medicine, known as Ayurveda has also used some form of Aromatherapy for over 3,000 years. Primitive perfumery probably began with the burning of gums and resins for incense. Eventually, richly scented plants were incorporated into animal and vegetable oils to anoint the body. Even in Neolithic times (7000-4000 BC) the fatty oils of olive and sesame were combined with fragrant plants to create ointments. Egyptian Papyrus manuscripts as old as 2700 BC has recorded the use of fragrant herbs, oils, perfumes and temple incense, and mentions healing ointments made of fragrant resins. The Epic of Gilgamesh tells of the legendary king of Ur in Mesopotamia (modern Iraq) burning incense made of cedar and myrrh to put the gods and goddesses into a pleasant mood. A tablet from neighboring Babylonia contains an import order for cedar, myrrh and cypress; another gives a recipe for scented ointments; a third suggests medicinal uses for cypress."[31]

[31] Joshua J. Mark, "Susa," Ancient History Encyclopedia (Ancient History Encyclopedia, November 2, 2019), https://www.ancient.eu/susa/.

10. Why is there a second harem for the King? (v. 14)

The narrative says that the King had a harem for virgins and a second harem for his concubines. If a virgin were not selected to be the queen, she would remain in the palace to serve the King as he decreed. There were two eunuchs in charge of the two harems. Thus, the virgins were kept separated from the concubines. Another possible reason for the two groups of women was so that women who went to be with the King could not pass along anything she learned that would please the King. Therefore it would be in the nature behavior of each woman that the King would base his decision.

11. Why is Esther's situation of guardianship repeated in verse fifteen?

The repetition could be that the author wanted to enforce the point that Esther was a Hebrew, not a Persian or Babylonian.

12. Why is the date important in verse sixteen?

"בַּחֹדֶשׁ הָעֲשִׂירִי הוּא חֹדֶשׁ טֵבֵת בִּשְׁנַת־שֶׁבַע לְמַלְכוּתוֹ, in the tenth month, the month of Tebeth, in the seventh year of his reign." The post-exilic community adopted the Babylonian names of the months of the lunar calendar (see *Vanderkam, ABD* 1:816). Tebeth, used only here in the OT corresponds to our December–January. Our narrator gives not a single hint why four years have elapsed since Vashti's deposal (see 1:3)—or what else might have transpired in the kingdom of Ahasuerus in this interval. Hence, the dating only suggests that Esther's victory came after a lengthy competition."[32]

---

[32] Bush, F. W. (1996). *Ruth, Esther* (Vol. 9, p. 366). Dallas: Word, Incorporated.

13. What is the second gathering of the virgins? (v. 19)

A possible answer is that there were other virgins in the harem who had not yet been seen by the King. Since the King selected Esther and made her the Queen, he did not need the rest of the virgins. The text does not indicate why the second gathering occurred. So, it is possible that the King dismissed the virgins. The virgins who spent the night with the King were in the second harem, the concubine harem.

14. Why is it essential that Mordecai was at the gate of the city? (v. 19)

Mordecai was at the gate indicating that he was either an officer of the government, and that is where his station was, or he was there attempting to discover how Esther was doing from the King's officials.

15. Why the repetition of Mordecai's instructions to Esther? (v. 20)

The Targum Rishon says that the King was asking Esther about her heritage. Esther did not give the King an answer, thus obeying Mordecai's instructions.

Biblical Personalities

1. Hadassah (v. 7) - This name was Esther's Hebrew name. The Targum Rishon says that her name was Hadassah because she was a righteous woman, and in those days, righteous people were compared to myrtle (*"hadas"* in Hebrew). She received the name Esther which comes from the name of a shining star which the Greeks called Astirah[33]. Esther was concealed in the home of Mordecai for seventy-five years, where she saw no man's face except that of Mordecai, who

---

[33] Astariah (Istera, from the Targum Sheni) was the name for the planet Venus.

became her nursing father. Esther was in her mother's womb when her father died. Her mother died upon giving birth to Hadassah. Mordecai took Hadassah into his house and called her his daughter.

"As for the name "Esther," determining its etymology adds nothing to the meaning of our story, though the subject has been much written about. It now seems most improbable that a name is a form of the Babylonian goddess Ishtar (cf. Clines, 287), given the graphic and onomastic evidence to the contrary expressed by Zadok (*ZAW* 98 [1986] 107). The other etymology most frequently suggested is the Persian word *stâra*, "star".[34]

2. Hegai – a eunuch in service to King Xerxes.

3. Mordecai - the son of Jair, the son of Shimei, the son of Kish, a Benjamite, who was the guardian of Esther.

4. Shaashgaz - the king's eunuch who was in charge of the concubines.

Phrase Study

1. אִישׁ יְהוּדִי הָיָה‎, "A Jewish man (there) was." Since the term יהודי‎ refers here to a man who was exiled from Judah with Jeconiah (or whose ancestor Kish was; see the discussion below), it could be rendered "Judean" (or even "Judahite"). But "Judean" (or "Judahite") properly refers to a member of the independent state of Judah, or in the period of the setting of our story to a member of the geographical area known by the same name, which was an

---

[34] Bush, F. W. (1996). *Ruth, Esther* (Vol. 9, p. 363). Dallas: Word, Incorporated.

administrative entity (perhaps something like a "sub-province"; cf. the books of Ezra-Nehemiah) of the Persian empire. But the epithet is used of Mordecai here and in five other passages (5:13; 6:10; 8:7; 9:31; 10:3; in my opinion the use in 9:29 is not original; see *Additional Note on vv 29–32 in Notes* to 9:6–32), and he is emphatically not a member of the Palestinian "Judean" community but rather one of the Judean/Judahite "diaspora," i.e., those who have not taken part in the restoration of the Judean community around Jerusalem but who live as expatriates in various localities in the Persian empire. This is transparent from the use of the denominative verb מתיהדים, lit. "became Jews" (8:17), which "signifies … something one can become without changing one's residence" (Levenson, *JES* 13 [1976] 450). The story is not about "Judeans" but about "Jews," i.e., members of the expatriate Jewish community dispersed throughout (2:8) the Persian empire. Hence, the epithet can only be rendered "Jew." The distinction is of the utmost importance for understanding the purpose and meaning of the whole narrative (see the discussion in *Theme and Purpose* in the *Introduction* to Esther)."[35]

2. וּבְהַגִּיעַ תֹּר נַעֲרָה וְנַעֲרָה לָבוֹא אֶל־הַמֶּלֶךְ אֲחַשְׁוֵרוֹשׁ, " "when the turn of each young woman came to enter to King Ahasuerus." It is striking that the idiom בול אל, "to go to," is used four times in vv 12–14 (12a, 13a, 14a, 14c), the detailed description of the manner in which each of the young women vied for the queenship. Given this frequency, the idiom may well be used with a double entendre. The passage is loaded with sensual implications, and this Hebrew idiom is a frequently used OT euphemism for sexual intercourse, used either

---

[35] Bush, F. W. (1996). *Ruth, Esther* (Vol. 9, p. 361). Dallas: Word, Incorporated.

of a man (e.g., Gen 16:2; 29:21, 23; 2 Sam 16:21, 22; Ruth 4:13; see esp. the *Comment* on Ruth 4:13) or a woman (e.g., 2 Sam 11:4)."[36]

3. וּמָרְדֳּכַי ישֵׁב בְּשַׁעַר־הַמֶּלֶךְ, " "Mordecai was sitting at the king's gate." The phrase might be taken literally, meaning that Mordecai was resorting to the palace area in order to hear further news of Esther's welfare (Clines, 281; cf. v 10). Most interpreters, however, understand the phrase in a figurative sense. Since the gate area was the place in the ancient Near East where the legal assembly met (see, e.g., Ruth 4) and business was conducted, the "king's gate" has come to mean "the royal court in general" (see Rüger, *Bib* 50 (1969) 247–50). This is made considerably more probable by the discovery of a monumental gate building comprising almost 13,000 square feet and situated some ninety yards east of the palace, unearthed by the French excavations of the 1970s (for a brief description with bibliography, see Yamauchi, *VT* 42 [1992] 274). Wehr (*Der Islam* 39 [1964] 247–60) has presented evidence from Herodotus and Xenophon as well as Assyrian and Babylonian royal inscriptions that such buildings housed the administrative and supply functions for the royal palace (for a brief description, see Heltzer, *BR* 8 [1992] 29; and for a more detailed treatment see Loretz, *WO* 4 [1967] 104–8). On the basis of this evidence, the expression "sitting in the king's gate" probably means "to hold an office in the palace administration" (see Loretz, *WO* 4 [1967] 104–8; Gordis, *JBL* 95 [1976] 47–48; Gordis' view, however, that the phrase refers specifically to a magistrate or judge seems too narrow an interpretation). This meaning of the term gives a better reason for the narrator's insertion of the following parenthesis (v 20) than does the literal understanding (note the significance of the reversal of the order of the phrase "parentage and nationality" from that in

---

[36] Bush, F. W. (1996). *Ruth, Esther* (Vol. 9, p. 365). Dallas: Word, Incorporated.

v 10). The literal rendering makes him virtually "an idler in the king's gate" (so Paton, 188). The reason for the mentioning of his position here is clear: his presence in the palace both gives him the opportunity to discover the plot against the king and permits him access to Esther to report it."[37]

Culture

Discussion

The form of execution in the Middle East was by crucifixion. Criminals were put on display so that the people could see them and become fearful about attempting to commit the same crime.[38]

Thoughts

Esther did not reveal her heritage to the eunuch or the King. If Esther had told them that she was Jewish, she would not have been able to save her people. Esther had to live with the knowledge that she could be executed at any time because of her deception. She did the work of the LORD, which was to save her people by marrying the King and took her place as the queen of the Empire. Esther did not know that she would become the salvation of Israel. How many people today are called into the service of the LORD without knowing what their end task would be? How many people are called by the LORD and never respond or perform the calling of the LORD?

---

[37] Bush, F. W. (1996). *Ruth, Esther* (Vol. 9, pp. 372–373). Dallas: Word, Incorporated.

[38] Rocco A. Errico and George M. Lamsa, *Aramaic Light on Ezra through the Song of Solomon* (Smyma, GA: Noohra Foundation, 2010).

Summary of the book of the Chronicles of the kings of Media and Persia

Original Persian document translated by Ti Burtzloff. Summary by Michael Koplitz

Chapter 1

When a woman who is given the charge of a wife fails to honor her husband's every request, she shall be cut off and put away from her husband, and he shall find another wife instead of the rebellious one.

Chapter 2

There was a young man who delivered the news to the provinces and became friends to a blind beggar named Mordechai, who was usually found at the Kingsgate. The blind beggar was concerned about who was going to marry his caregiver. The delivery boy met Mordechai's caregiver, Hadassah. The delivery boy wanted to marry Hadassah, but he feared that he could not provide for her if she were to become his bride. The delivery boy lusted for Hadassah and created a plot to marry her to satisfy his lustful cravings. He knew that they could not afford to have a child, so he conceived of a plan to spill his seed on the ground when he was with Hadassah on their wedding night.

So when the delivery boy was with Hadassah for the first time and engaged in sexual intercourse, he spilled his seed on the ground, and this act caused the delivery boy to fall on his seed and die on top of it (God was not pleased that the boy did this). Hadassah told her uncle Mordechai what happened. She did not know what to do because the delivery boy brought messages to the king about what was happening in the kingdom. Mordechai sent Hadassah to report the news of the death of the delivery boy to King Ahasuerus. She barged into the king's sleeping quarters to tell him this news. When she did so, she laughed at the king. The king was going to have Hadassah publicly executed for her intrusion. Hadassah told the king that the delivery boy had died when they were together. The king did not believe her and sent people out looking for the delivery boy.

Chapter 3

King Ahasuerus mocked Hadassah for two days. On the third day, the king became worried about what happened to his delivery boy. He decided to believe Hadassah's story, and he took her hand and begged for her forgiveness. The king then asked how old Hadassah was. She replied that she was 15 years old. The king asked Hadassah what her name was, for he did not know her name. King Ahasuerus decided to take Hadassah as his wife. The king suggested that he should pay a respectful visit to the uncle of Hadassah and ask for the blessings of the uncle for the king to take the young Hadassah as a bride. Hadassah explained to the king that he did not need permission from Mordechai to marry her.

So Hadassah went into the king but told him that her name was Esther, not Hadassah. Hadassah did not want to risk the possibility of the king discovering that she was a Hebrew because she feared that information could get her killed. Hadassah told the king that Mordechai was her cousin, and that is why the king did not need his approval to marry her.

Chapter 4

The king fell deeply in love with Esther shortly after they married. The king had stumbled on to the great powers of God when he fell deeply in love with Esther. King Ahasuerus was filled with joy because of Esther, and he gave all his wealth to the needy of his kingdom. The king left the palace and went out into the streets and clothed the naked and gave food to the hungry, and gave drink on to the thirsty. The king started to perform healings in the kingdom when he saw the blind beggar Mordechai. So the king healed Mordechai of his blindness. The king then invited Mordechai to live with him in the palace. When Mordechai came to the palace, Esther explained everything to him that had transpired so that he would not say anything to the king that might reveal any of the lies that Esther initially told unto her husband, King.

Chapter 5

The king and Mordechai became great friends. Mordechai told the king the whole truth about Esther. Mordechai told the king that Esther was Hadassah and that he was her uncle, not her cousin. Mordechai explained to the king that he never taught his young niece Hadassah the courteous manner to approach a great king and that she knew not what she was doing. The fear of her own life caused her to create falsehoods because she desired to live as opposed to being publicly executed.

Chapter 6

A man of his word came from the forest in order to shine light upon the great King. This occurred when Hadassah was 17 years old. For the king had become self-righteous because he had healed so many and help so many people that he had developed blindness and became arrogant and became lost under the spell of his adverse ego. The man from the forest said that he came from the tribe of prophets. He said to the king that he had come to spare the king from the same fate that fell upon the legendary strongman named Samson. He told the king that the woman that he had fallen in love with were two different women. The man told the king that when he was away she became Hadassah, and she did not identify with Queen Esther during the times that she perceived herself as Hadassah, for she loved the man that her uncle Mordechai had chosen for her to marry. The man Mordechai had picked for Hadassah to marry was the delivery boy.

The king asked the prophet what his name was. He responded to Grand Master Haman, king of the swamp. Grand Master Haman said that he would never be a king over people for every person who needs to be king over themselves.

Chapter 7

The king asked the swamp man how he was able to obtain his wisdom. Grand Master Haman said that they needed to climb a particular mountain to the top, and there he would receive the wisdom. So the king brought chariots together, and Grand Master Haman, King Ahasuerus, Queen Esther, and Mordechai left for the mountain. When they reached the top of the mountain, Esther asked what this place was? The swamp man answered Esther saying, this place, my love, is the head of the volcano. Esther became offended that the swamp man called her his love because she was a married Queen. The swamp man smiled and called her Hadassah. When he called her Hadassah, she immediately realized that she hated the king. The swamp man also said that Mordechai was never blind. Instead, it was just a hustle.

The swamp man showed Esther the secrets of the past kings, present kings, and future kings in one of the caves at the top of the mountain.

Chapter 8

The swamp man and Hadassah remained in the magical mountains for all of their days until the volcano erupted and consumed their tabernacles of flesh. Mordechai had returned safely to the city and began writing many articles about having inherited all the wealth of the king. Mordechai dwelt in the king's palace, but he never had anyone call him king. Mordechai missed his beloved niece Hadassah. He wrote a book about her in order to help him cope with her absence. He called it the book of Esther. Thereby naming the book in honor of her bravery. Mordechai slept with this book under his pillow for the rest of his life.

Chapter Three

Language

New American Standard 1995	Hebrew
[1] After these events King Ahasuerus promoted Haman, the son of Hammedatha the Agagite, and advanced him and established his authority over all the princes who *were* with him. [2] All the king's servants who were at the king's gate bowed down and paid homage to Haman; for so the king had commanded concerning him. But Mordecai neither bowed down nor paid homage. [3] Then the king's servants who were at the king's gate said to Mordecai, "Why are you transgressing the king's command?" [4] Now it was when they had spoken daily to him and he would not listen to them, that they told Haman to see whether Mordecai's reason would stand; for he had told them that he was a Jew. [5] When Haman saw that Mordecai neither bowed down nor paid homage to him, Haman was filled with rage. [6] But he disdained to lay hands on Mordecai alone, for they had told him *who* the people of Mordecai *were*; therefore Haman sought to destroy all the Jews, the people of Mordecai, who *were* throughout the whole kingdom of Ahasuerus. [7] In the first month, which is the month Nisan, in the twelfth year of King	אַחַר הַדְּבָרִים הָאֵלֶּה גִּדַּל הַמֶּלֶךְ אֲחַשְׁוֵרוֹשׁ אֶת־הָמָן בֶּן־הַמְּדָתָא הָאֲגָגִי וַיְנַשְּׂאֵהוּ וַיָּשֶׂם אֶת־כִּסְאוֹ מֵעַל כָּל־הַשָּׂרִים אֲשֶׁר אִתּוֹ: 2 וְכָל־עַבְדֵי הַמֶּלֶךְ אֲשֶׁר־בְּשַׁעַר הַמֶּלֶךְ כֹּרְעִים וּמִשְׁתַּחֲוִים לְהָמָן כִּי־כֵן צִוָּה־לוֹ הַמֶּלֶךְ וּמָרְדֳּכַי לֹא יִכְרַע וְלֹא יִשְׁתַּחֲוֶה: 3 וַיֹּאמְרוּ עַבְדֵי הַמֶּלֶךְ אֲשֶׁר־בְּשַׁעַר הַמֶּלֶךְ לְמָרְדֳּכָי מַדּוּעַ אַתָּה עוֹבֵר אֵת מִצְוַת הַמֶּלֶךְ: 4 וַיְהִי (בְּאָמְרָם) [כְּאָמְרָם] אֵלָיו יוֹם וָיוֹם וְלֹא שָׁמַע אֲלֵיהֶם וַיַּגִּידוּ לְהָמָן לִרְאוֹת הֲיַעַמְדוּ דִּבְרֵי מָרְדֳּכַי כִּי־הִגִּיד לָהֶם אֲשֶׁר־הוּא יְהוּדִי: 5 וַיַּרְא הָמָן כִּי־אֵין מָרְדֳּכַי כֹּרֵעַ וּמִשְׁתַּחֲוֶה לוֹ וַיִּמָּלֵא הָמָן חֵמָה: 6 וַיִּבֶז בְּעֵינָיו לִשְׁלֹחַ יָד בְּמָרְדֳּכַי לְבַדּוֹ כִּי־הִגִּידוּ לוֹ אֶת־עַם מָרְדֳּכָי וַיְבַקֵּשׁ הָמָן לְהַשְׁמִיד אֶת־כָּל־הַיְּהוּדִים אֲשֶׁר בְּכָל־מַלְכוּת אֲחַשְׁוֵרוֹשׁ עַם מָרְדֳּכָי: 7 בַּחֹדֶשׁ הָרִאשׁוֹן הוּא־חֹדֶשׁ נִיסָן בִּשְׁנַת שְׁתֵּים עֶשְׂרֵה לַמֶּלֶךְ אֲחַשְׁוֵרוֹשׁ הִפִּיל פּוּר הוּא הַגּוֹרָל לִפְנֵי הָמָן מִיּוֹם לְיוֹם וּמֵחֹדֶשׁ לְחֹדֶשׁ שְׁנֵים־עָשָׂר הוּא־חֹדֶשׁ אֲדָר: ס 8 וַיֹּאמֶר הָמָן לַמֶּלֶךְ אֲחַשְׁוֵרוֹשׁ יֶשְׁנוֹ עַם־אֶחָד מְפֻזָּר וּמְפֹרָד בֵּין הָעַמִּים בְּכֹל מְדִינוֹת מַלְכוּתֶךָ וְדָתֵיהֶם שֹׁנוֹת מִכָּל־עָם וְאֶת־דָּתֵי הַמֶּלֶךְ אֵינָם עֹשִׂים וְלַמֶּלֶךְ אֵין־שֹׁוֶה לְהַנִּיחָם: 9 אִם־עַל־הַמֶּלֶךְ טוֹב יִכָּתֵב לְאַבְּדָם וַעֲשֶׂרֶת אֲלָפִים כִּכַּר־כֶּסֶף אֶשְׁקוֹל עַל־יְדֵי עֹשֵׂי הַמְּלָאכָה לְהָבִיא אֶל־גִּנְזֵי הַמֶּלֶךְ:

Ahasuerus, Pur, that is the lot, was cast before Haman from day to day and from month *to month*, until the twelfth month, that is the month Adar.

8 Then Haman said to King Ahasuerus, "There is a certain people scattered and dispersed among the peoples in all the provinces of your kingdom; their laws are different from *those* of all *other* people and they do not observe the king's laws, so it is not in the king's interest to let them remain.

9 "If it is pleasing to the king, let it be decreed that they be destroyed, and I will pay ten thousand talents of silver into the hands of those who carry on the *king's* business, to put into the king's treasuries."

10 Then the king took his signet ring from his hand and gave it to Haman, the son of Hammedatha the Agagite, the enemy of the Jews.

11 The king said to Haman, "The silver is yours, and the people *also*, to do with them as you please."

12 Then the king's scribes were summoned on the thirteenth day of the first month, and it was written just as Haman commanded to the king's satraps, to the governors who were over each province and to the princes of each people, each province according to its script, each people according to its language, being written in the name of King Ahasuerus and sealed with the king's signet ring.

13 Letters were sent by couriers to all the king's provinces to destroy, to kill and to annihilate all the Jews, both young and old, women and children, in one day, the thirteenth *day* of the twelfth month,

10 וַיָּ֨סַר הַמֶּ֤לֶךְ אֶת־טַבַּעְתּוֹ֙ מֵעַ֣ל יָד֔וֹ וַֽיִּתְּנָ֔הּ לְהָמָ֛ן בֶּֽן־הַמְּדָ֥תָא הָאֲגָגִ֖י צֹרֵ֥ר הַיְּהוּדִֽים׃

11 וַיֹּ֤אמֶר הַמֶּ֙לֶךְ֙ לְהָמָ֔ן הַכֶּ֖סֶף נָת֣וּן לָ֑ךְ וְהָעָ֕ם לַעֲשׂ֥וֹת בּ֖וֹ כַּטּ֥וֹב בְּעֵינֶֽיךָ׃

12 וַיִּקָּרְא֣וּ סֹפְרֵ֣י הַמֶּ֡לֶךְ בַּחֹ֣דֶשׁ הָרִאשׁ֡וֹן בִּשְׁלוֹשָׁה֩ עָשָׂ֨ר יוֹם֜ בּ֗וֹ וַיִּכָּתֵ֣ב כְּֽכָל־אֲשֶׁר־צִוָּ֣ה הָמָ֡ן אֶ֣ל אֲחַשְׁדַּרְפְּנֵֽי־הַ֠מֶּלֶךְ וְֽאֶל־הַפַּחוֹת֩ אֲשֶׁ֨ר ׀ עַל־מְדִינָ֜ה וּמְדִינָ֗ה וְאֶל־שָׂ֤רֵי עַם֙ וָעָ֔ם מְדִינָ֤ה וּמְדִינָה֙ כִּכְתָבָ֔הּ וְעַ֥ם וָעָ֖ם כִּלְשׁוֹנ֑וֹ בְּשֵׁ֨ם הַמֶּ֤לֶךְ אֲחַשְׁוֵרֹשׁ֙ נִכְתָּ֔ב וְנֶחְתָּ֖ם בְּטַבַּ֥עַת הַמֶּֽלֶךְ׃

13 וְנִשְׁל֨וֹחַ סְפָרִ֜ים בְּיַ֣ד הָרָצִים֮ אֶל־כָּל־מְדִינ֣וֹת הַמֶּלֶךְ֒ לְהַשְׁמִ֡יד לַהֲרֹ֣ג וּלְאַבֵּ֣ד אֶת־כָּל־הַ֠יְּהוּדִים מִנַּ֨עַר וְעַד־זָקֵ֜ן טַ֤ף וְנָשִׁים֙ בְּי֣וֹם אֶחָ֔ד בִּשְׁלוֹשָׁ֥ה עָשָׂ֛ר לְחֹ֥דֶשׁ שְׁנֵים־עָשָׂ֖ר הוּא־חֹ֣דֶשׁ אֲדָ֑ר וּשְׁלָלָ֖ם לָבֽוֹז׃

14 פַּתְשֶׁ֣גֶן הַכְּתָ֗ב לְהִנָּ֤תֵֽן דָּת֙ בְּכָל־מְדִינָ֣ה וּמְדִינָ֔ה גָּל֖וּי לְכָל־הָֽעַמִּ֑ים לִהְי֥וֹת עֲתִדִ֖ים לַיּ֥וֹם הַזֶּֽה׃

15 הָרָצִ֞ים יָצְא֤וּ דְחוּפִים֙ בִּדְבַ֣ר הַמֶּ֔לֶךְ וְהַדָּ֥ת נִתְּנָ֖ה בְּשׁוּשַׁ֣ן הַבִּירָ֑ה וְהַמֶּ֤לֶךְ וְהָמָן֙ יָשְׁב֣וּ לִשְׁתּ֔וֹת וְהָעִ֥יר שׁוּשָׁ֖ן נָבֽוֹכָה׃ פ

| which is the month Adar, and to seize their possessions as plunder.

[14] A copy of the edict to be issued as law in every province was published to all the peoples so that they should be ready for this day.

[15] The couriers went out impelled by the king's command while the decree was issued at the citadel in Susa; and while the king and Haman sat down to drink, the city of Susa was in confusion. | |

Process of Discovery

Linguistics Section

Linguistic Structure

A [1] After these events King Ahasuerus promoted Haman, the son of Hammedatha the Agagite, and advanced him and established his authority over all the princes who *were* with him.

> **B** [2] All the king's servants who were at the king's gate bowed down and paid homage to Haman; for so the king had commanded concerning him. But Mordecai neither bowed down nor paid homage. [3] Then the king's servants who were at the king's gate said to Mordecai, "Why are you transgressing the king's command?" [4] Now it was when they had spoken daily to him and he would not listen to them, that they told Haman to see whether Mordecai's reason would stand; for he had told them that he was a Jew. [5] When Haman saw that Mordecai neither bowed down nor paid homage to him, Haman was filled with rage. [6] But he disdained to lay hands on Mordecai alone, for they had told him *who* the people of Mordecai *were*; therefore Haman sought to destroy all the Jews, the people of Mordecai, who *were* throughout the whole kingdom of Ahasuerus. [7] In the first month, which is the month Nisan, in the twelfth year of King Ahasuerus, Pur, that is the lot, was cast before Haman from day to day and from month *to month*, until the twelfth month, that is the month Adar.

> **C** [8] Then Haman said to King Ahasuerus, "There is a certain people scattered and dispersed among the peoples in all the provinces of your kingdom; their laws are different from *those* of all *other* people and they do not observe the king's laws, so it is not in the king's interest to let them remain. [9] "If it is pleasing to the king, let it be decreed that they be destroyed, and I will pay ten thousand talents of silver into the hands of those who carry on the *king's* business, to put into the king's treasuries." [10] Then the king took his signet ring from his hand and gave it to Haman, the son of Hammedatha the Agagite, the enemy of the Jews. [11] The king said to Haman, "The silver is yours, and the people *also*, to do with them as you please."

B' [12] Then the king's scribes were summoned on the thirteenth day of the first month, and it was written just as Haman commanded to the king's satraps, to the governors who were over each province and to the princes of each people, each province according to its script, each people according to its language, being written in the name of King Ahasuerus and sealed with the king's signet ring. [13] Letters were sent by couriers to all the king's provinces to destroy, to kill and to annihilate all the Jews, both young and old, women and children, in one day, the thirteenth *day* of the twelfth month, which is the month Adar, and to seize their possessions as plunder. [14] A copy of the edict to be issued as law in every province was published to all the peoples so that they should be ready for this day.

A' [15] The couriers went out impelled by the king's command while the decree was issued at the citadel in Susa; and while the king and Haman sat down to drink, the city of Susa was in confusion.

Discussion

This chapter forms an A-B-C chiasm. The center of the chiasm is the treachery of Haman.

Questioning the Passage

1. Why did Ahasuerus promote Haman? (v. 1)

   According to the Targum Rishon, the LORD did not want to destroy Haman as long as he was unknown. When Haman became known to the world and influential, the LORD said that Haman would be punished for all the oppression his ancestors caused Israel to endure. [39]

2. Why did Mordecai not bow down to Haman? (v. 2)

   The Targum Rishon says that Haman had an image on his chest. Mordechai refused to bow down before the image. [40] The image must have been a depiction

---

[39] "The Aramaic Bible, the Two Targums of Esther" The Liturgical Press. 1991
[40] IBID.

of a Persian or some other pagan god. Mordecai placed his faith and obedience to the LORD above his obedience to the order of King Ahasuerus.

Culturally bowing down to Haman also meant to offer worshp to him. Mordechai being a Hebrew, could only worship the LORD.[41]

3. Why did Haman want to destroy the Jews in Persia? (v. 6)

Haman inquired who Mordechai was. When he learned that Mordechai was a descendant of Jacob, Haman became determined to avenge his ancestor Esau. The descendants of Esau believed that Jacob had stolen the birthright from Esau. Haman's act was an act of revenge.

4. Why did Haman cast lots to determine when the edict would be carried out? (v. 7)

"Because he was attempting to break what, to his mind, was a "vicious cycle" that had been plaguing him and his ilk since the appearance of the Jewish nation a thousand years earlier. Many great and powerful men, from Pharaoh to Nebuchadnezzar—not to mention Haman's own ancestors, the Amalekites— had tried to destroy this people."[42] He used luck to determine the date instead of picking a date. This method worked out for the Hebrews because it gave them time to repent of their sins and to prepare for the day, that is, to work out a defense.

---

[41] Rocco A. Errico and George M. Lamsa, *Aramaic Light on Ezra through the Song of Solomon* (Smyma, GA: Noohra Foundation, 2010).
[42] Yanki Tauber, "A Throw of Dice," Judaism, February 29, 2000, https://www.chabad.org/holidays/purim/article_cdo/aid/1404/jewish/A-Throw-of-Dice.htm. Accessed November 11, 2019.

5. What did Haman mean about the Hebrew laws being different? (v. 8)

    The Targum Rishon says that Haman told King Ahasuerus that the Hebrew people did not eat the same food as the people of the Empire did. The Hebrews celebrated holidays that were different from the Persian holidays. The Targum Sheni describes all of the yearly holidays and festivals that the Hebrew people celebrated in Persia.[43]

6. Is there a significance to the date of Nissan 13? (v. 12)

    The first month of the year is the month of Nissan. Nissan 14 is the preparation day for the Passover, Nissan 15 is the first day of Passover. The Hebrew people received salvation from the grip of Egypt on Nissan 14th because it was on that day that the angel of death came over Egypt and killed the first-born sons. Perhaps Mordecai used this event, the day before the Passover preparation, to remind the people that the LORD would offer salvation as long as they repented from their sins. They had almost one year to prepare themselves for the LORD's salvation. The Passover event demonstrated the LORD's love for His chosen people. They were in Persia because of the sins of the past. They needed the LORD's redemptive power to save them from annihilation. Passover seems like an excellent time to start the repentance process.

---

[43] "The Aramaic Bible, the Two Targums of Esther" The Liturgical Press. 1991

7. Why was the city of Susa in confusion? (v. 15)

The Targum Rishon says that the city was in confusion because the gentiles of the city were rejoicing over the King's edict while the people of the House of Israel were weeping. [44]

Biblical Personalities

1. Haman – he was the son of Hammedatha, who was the descendant of Agag, son of Amalek. The Targum Sheni offers a genealogy of Haman, which goes back to Esau.[45] "According to the Bible, Amalek was the first enemy that Israel encountered after the crossing of the Sea of Reeds."[46] Israel and the Amalekites (descendants of Amalek) clashed throughout the centuries. Hebrews who believe in reincarnation believe that Haman was the reincarnation of Amalek.

Phrase Study

1. פוּר (pûr) lot. "The word occurs only in the book of Esther (3:7; 9:24; 9:26 (two times), 9:28, 29, 31, 32). Hebrew פוּר is to be distinguished from גּוֹרָל, the usual word for "lot." In 3:7 and 9:24 the two words appear beside each other.

It appears obvious that פוּר is related to Babylonian pūru which means "lot" and secondarily "fate." Of special interest is that in 9:26, 28, 29, 31, 32 the Hebrew "Purim" is translated in the LXX by φρουραι, from a verb meaning "to watch, guard." One suggestion has been to see in φρουραι the aramaized from of Babylonian purruru "to destroy, exterminate." (Lewy). From 9:20–28

---

[44] IBID.
[45] "The Aramaic Bible, the Two Targums of Esther" The Liturgical Press. 1991
[46] "Ancient Jewish History," The Amalekites, accessed November 19, 2019, https://www.jewishvirtuallibrary.org/the-amalekites.

we learn that Purim was a feast instituted by Mordecai to celebrate the deliverance of Jews from Haman's plot to kill them. The observance of Purim was determined after lots were cast by Haman in order to determine the month in which the slaughter was to take place. Est 3:7 says that Haman, having already decided on the pogrom, consulted the lots only to learn the most propitious day on which to extirpate the race of Mordecai. The LXX adds to the MT these words, "And the lot fell on the fourteenth of the month called Adar" (March/April); that is, the decree was to be enforced almost a full year after its original promulgation. One asks, why did Haman send the edict out almost twelve months in advance of the proposed day of slaughter? Is it reading in too much to see in this unusual arrangement the sovereign hand of God once again protecting his children, even though they are in exile?"[47]

Thoughts

Vengeance is something that dies hard and sometimes never dies. Haman wanted vengeance for an event that happened centuries earlier. The event of Jacob obtaining the birthright from Esau was probably a turning point for Esau's descendants. The story of Jacob and Esau in Genesis says that when Jacob left Laban and met Esau that Esau had forgiven him and the brothers reunited. Even though the two brothers came together the descendants of Esau never forgave the descendants of Jacob. Amalek, a descendant of Esau, attacked Israel when they came out of Egypt and were in the Sinai desert. Throughout the centuries, until the Romans destroyed Esau's descendants, they attempted to destroy Israel. The LORD protected His chosen people and never allowed Esau's descendants to destroy Israel. The LORD will always

---

[47] Lewy, J., "The Feast on the 14th Day of Adar," HUCA 14: 127–51. Lindblom, J., "Lot-Casting in the Old Testament, "VT 12 164–78. Moore, C., in AB, Esther, pp, XLVI-XLIX.. Feinberg, C. L. "Purim" ZPEB, IV, 957–58.

protect those who belong to the LORD. The LORD expects His people to live by the commandments found in the Torah and Prophets.

Chapter Four

Language

New American Standard 1995	Hebrew
[1] When Mordecai learned all that had been done, he tore his clothes, put on sackcloth and ashes, and went out into the midst of the city and wailed loudly and bitterly. [2] He went as far as the king's gate, for no one was to enter the king's gate clothed in sackcloth. [3] In each and every province where the command and decree of the king came, there was great mourning among the Jews, with fasting, weeping and wailing; and many lay on sackcloth and ashes. [4] Then Esther's maidens and her eunuchs came and told her, and the queen writhed in great anguish. And she sent garments to clothe Mordecai that he might remove his sackcloth from him, but he did not accept *them*. [5] Then Esther summoned Hathach from the king's eunuchs, whom the king had appointed to attend her, and ordered him *to go* to Mordecai to learn what this *was* and why it *was*. [6] So Hathach went out to Mordecai to the city square in front of the king's gate. [7] Mordecai told him all that had happened to him, and the exact amount of money that Haman had promised to	וּמָרְדֳּכַי יָדַע אֶת־כָּל־אֲשֶׁר נַעֲשָׂה וַיִּקְרַע מָרְדֳּכַי אֶת־בְּגָדָיו וַיִּלְבַּשׁ שַׂק וָאֵפֶר וַיֵּצֵא בְּתוֹךְ הָעִיר וַיִּזְעַק זְעָקָה גְדֹלָה וּמָרָה׃ וַיָּבוֹא עַד לִפְנֵי שַׁעַר־הַמֶּלֶךְ כִּי אֵין לָבוֹא אֶל־שַׁעַר הַמֶּלֶךְ בִּלְבוּשׁ שָׂק׃ וּבְכָל־מְדִינָה וּמְדִינָה מְקוֹם אֲשֶׁר דְּבַר־הַמֶּלֶךְ וְדָתוֹ מַגִּיעַ אֵבֶל גָּדוֹל לַיְּהוּדִים וְצוֹם וּבְכִי וּמִסְפֵּד שַׂק וָאֵפֶר יֻצַּע לָרַבִּים׃ וַתָּבוֹאינָה נַעֲרוֹת אֶסְתֵּר וְסָרִיסֶיהָ וַיַּגִּידוּ לָהּ וַתִּתְחַלְחַל הַמַּלְכָּה מְאֹד וַתִּשְׁלַח בְּגָדִים לְהַלְבִּישׁ אֶת־מָרְדֳּכַי וּלְהָסִיר שַׂקּוֹ מֵעָלָיו וְלֹא קִבֵּל׃ וַתִּקְרָא אֶסְתֵּר לַהֲתָךְ מִסָּרִיסֵי הַמֶּלֶךְ אֲשֶׁר הֶעֱמִיד לְפָנֶיהָ וַתְּצַוֵּהוּ עַל־מָרְדֳּכָי לָדַעַת מַה־זֶּה וְעַל־מַה־זֶּה׃ וַיֵּצֵא הֲתָךְ אֶל־מָרְדֳּכָי אֶל־רְחוֹב הָעִיר אֲשֶׁר לִפְנֵי שַׁעַר־הַמֶּלֶךְ׃ וַיַּגֶּד־לוֹ מָרְדֳּכַי אֵת כָּל־אֲשֶׁר קָרָהוּ וְאֵת פָּרָשַׁת הַכֶּסֶף אֲשֶׁר אָמַר הָמָן לִשְׁקוֹל עַל־גִּנְזֵי הַמֶּלֶךְ (בַּיְּהוּדִיִּים) [בַּיְּהוּדִים] לְאַבְּדָם׃ וְאֶת־פַּתְשֶׁגֶן כְּתָב־הַדָּת אֲשֶׁר־נִתַּן בְּשׁוּשָׁן לְהַשְׁמִידָם נָתַן לוֹ לְהַרְאוֹת אֶת־אֶסְתֵּר וּלְהַגִּיד לָהּ וּלְצַוּוֹת עָלֶיהָ לָבוֹא אֶל־הַמֶּלֶךְ לְהִתְחַנֶּן־לוֹ וּלְבַקֵּשׁ מִלְּפָנָיו עַל־עַמָּהּ׃ וַיָּבוֹא הֲתָךְ וַיַּגֵּד לְאֶסְתֵּר אֵת דִּבְרֵי מָרְדֳּכָי׃ וַתֹּאמֶר אֶסְתֵּר לַהֲתָךְ וַתְּצַוֵּהוּ אֶל־מָרְדֳּכָי׃ כָּל־עַבְדֵי הַמֶּלֶךְ וְעַם־מְדִינוֹת הַמֶּלֶךְ יוֹדְעִים אֲשֶׁר כָּל־אִישׁ וְאִשָּׁה אֲשֶׁר יָבוֹא־אֶל־הַמֶּלֶךְ אֶל־הֶחָצֵר הַפְּנִימִית אֲשֶׁר לֹא־יִקָּרֵא

pay to the king's treasuries for the destruction of the Jews.

8 He also gave him a copy of the text of the edict which had been issued in Susa for their destruction, that he might show Esther and inform her, and to order her to go in to the king to implore his favor and to plead with him for her people.

9 Hathach came back and related Mordecai's words to Esther.

10 Then Esther spoke to Hathach and ordered him *to reply* to Mordecai:

11 "All the king's servants and the people of the king's provinces know that for any man or woman who comes to the king to the inner court who is not summoned, he has but one law, that he be put to death, unless the king holds out to him the golden scepter so that he may live. And I have not been summoned to come to the king for these thirty days."

12 They related Esther's words to Mordecai.

13 Then Mordecai told *them* to reply to Esther, "Do not imagine that you in the king's palace can escape any more than all the Jews.

14 "For if you remain silent at this time, relief and deliverance will arise for the Jews from another place and you and your father's house will perish. And who knows whether you have not attained royalty for such a time as this?"

15 Then Esther told *them* to reply to Mordecai,

16 "Go, assemble all the Jews who are found in Susa, and fast for me; do not eat or drink for three days, night or day. I and my maidens also will fast in the same way. And thus I will go in to the king, which is

אַחַת דָּתוֹ לְהָמִית לְבַד מֵאֲשֶׁר יוֹשִׁיט־לוֹ הַמֶּלֶךְ אֶת־שַׁרְבִיט הַזָּהָב וְחָיָה וַאֲנִי לֹא נִקְרֵאתִי לָבוֹא אֶל־הַמֶּלֶךְ זֶה שְׁלוֹשִׁים יוֹם:

12 וַיַּגִּידוּ לְמָרְדֳּכָי אֵת דִּבְרֵי אֶסְתֵּר: פ

13 וַיֹּאמֶר מָרְדֳּכַי לְהָשִׁיב אֶל־אֶסְתֵּר אַל־תְּדַמִּי בְנַפְשֵׁךְ לְהִמָּלֵט בֵּית־הַמֶּלֶךְ מִכָּל־הַיְּהוּדִים:

14 כִּי אִם־הַחֲרֵשׁ תַּחֲרִישִׁי בָּעֵת הַזֹּאת רֶוַח וְהַצָּלָה יַעֲמוֹד לַיְּהוּדִים מִמָּקוֹם אַחֵר וְאַתְּ וּבֵית־אָבִיךְ תֹּאבֵדוּ וּמִי יוֹדֵעַ אִם־לְעֵת כָּזֹאת הִגַּעַתְּ לַמַּלְכוּת:

15 וַתֹּאמֶר אֶסְתֵּר לְהָשִׁיב אֶל־מָרְדֳּכָי:

16 לֵךְ כְּנוֹס אֶת־כָּל־הַיְּהוּדִים הַנִּמְצְאִים בְּשׁוּשָׁן וְצוּמוּ עָלַי וְאַל־תֹּאכְלוּ וְאַל־תִּשְׁתּוּ שְׁלֹשֶׁת יָמִים לַיְלָה וָיוֹם גַּם־אֲנִי וְנַעֲרֹתַי אָצוּם כֵּן וּבְכֵן אָבוֹא אֶל־הַמֶּלֶךְ אֲשֶׁר לֹא־כַדָּת וְכַאֲשֶׁר אָבַדְתִּי אָבָדְתִּי:

17 וַיַּעֲבֹר מָרְדֳּכָי וַיַּעַשׂ כְּכֹל אֲשֶׁר־צִוְּתָה עָלָיו אֶסְתֵּר: ס

not according to the law; and if I perish, I perish." [17] So Mordecai went away and did just as Esther had commanded him.	

Process of Discovery

Linguistics Section

Linguistic Structure

[Acts of Mordecai] [1] When Mordecai learned all that had been done, he tore his clothes, put on sackcloth and ashes, and went out into the midst of the city and wailed loudly and bitterly. [2] He went as far as the king's gate, for no one was to enter the king's gate clothed in sackcloth. [3] In each and every province where the command and decree of the king came, there was great mourning among the Jews, with fasting, weeping and wailing; and many lay on sackcloth and ashes.

[Message of Esther] [4] Then Esther's maidens and her eunuchs came and told her, and the queen writhed in great anguish. And she sent garments to clothe Mordecai that he might remove his sackcloth from him, but he did not accept *them*. [5] Then Esther summoned Hathach from the king's eunuchs, whom the king had appointed to attend her, and ordered him *to go* to Mordecai to learn what this *was* and why it *was*.

[Request of Mordecai] [6] So Hathach went out to Mordecai to the city square in front of the king's gate. [7] Mordecai told him all that had happened to him, and the exact amount of money that Haman had promised to pay to the king's treasuries for the destruction of the Jews. [8] He also gave him a copy of the text of the edict which had been issued in Susa for their destruction, that he might show Esther and inform her, and to order her to go in to the king to implore his favor and to plead with him for her people. [9] Hathach came back and related Mordecai's words to Esther.

[Message from Esther] [10] Then Esther spoke to Hathach and ordered him *to reply* to Mordecai: [11] "All the king's servants and the people of the king's provinces know that for any man or woman who comes to the king to the inner court who is not summoned, he has but one law, that he be put to death, unless the king holds out to him the golden scepter so that he may live. And I have not been summoned to come to the king for these thirty days." ¹² They related Esther's words to Mordecai.

[Request of Mordecai] ¹³ Then Mordecai told *them* to reply to Esther, "Do not imagine that you in the king's palace can escape any more than all the Jews. ¹⁴ "For if you remain silent at this time, relief and deliverance will arise for the Jews from another place and you and your father's house will perish. And who knows whether you have not attained royalty for such a time as this?"

[Message of Esther] ¹⁵ Then Esther told *them* to reply to Mordecai, ¹⁶ "Go, assemble all the Jews who are found in Susa, and fast for me; do not eat or drink for three days, night or day. I and my maidens also will fast in the same way. And thus I will go in to the king, which is not according to the law; and if I perish, I perish."

[Acts of Mordecai] ¹⁷ So Mordecai went away and did just as Esther had commanded him.

Discussion

This chapter is the conversation through messengers between Mordecai and Esther. Mordecai needed to tell Esther about what the King's edict was. He reminded her that she was a Jew and would be caught in the same fate as her fellow Jews.

Questioning the Passage

1. How did Mordecai learn about the plot to kill the Jews? (v. 1)
    According to the Targum Sheni, the LORD sent Elijah the high priest to tell Mordecai that he needed to pray before the LORD for the people. A heavenly decree was made against the House of Israel, and King Ahasuerus was going to

carry it out. The heavenly decree occurred because the Jews in Susa partook of King Ahasuerus' seven-day feast.[48]

2. Why did Mordecai tear his clothes, put on sackcloth and ashes? (v. 1)
    The Targum Sheni says that Mordecai was so upset over the divine decree that he removed his clothing by tearing them off his body and he covered himself with sackcloth. What was the most upsetting was that the decree was to kill all of God's people in the Empire, not a small number, or even half, but rather the entire population.[49]

3. Why was it not legal to wear sackcloth in the King's gate? (v. 2)
    This was a law made by the King. The Targum Sheni says that Mordecai went to the King's gate anyway because the decree ordering the death of all Jews in the Empire was posted in the gateway. Mordecai went there every day to weep for his people.[50]

4. Why did Esther send clothes to Mordecai? (v. 4)
    An explanation is that if Mordecai continually came to the gate in sackcloth that a guard at the gate would eventually arrest him. Mordecai would have been questioned and possibly tortured. He could have given away Esther's deception, which would have had both of them killed.

5. Why did Mordecai reject the clothing from Esther? (v. 4)

---

[48] "The Aramaic Bible, the Two Targums of Esther" The Liturgical Press. 1991
[49] IBID.
[50] IBID.

Mordecai was so upset about the decree that he would not accept Esther's clothing gift. He wanted it to be clear to the people in the King's gate that he was a Jew and was going to be murdered. Perhaps Mordecai felt that he could get a sympathy following who could speak to the King.

6. Is there a significance to Esther not being called to the King in thirty days (v. 11)

The significance is number thirty. Thirty is considered a time for preparation. "The impact of an event in the Jewish calendar can be felt thirty days before its arrival."[51] Esther had thirty days to learn the laws of the land. The one law that she used was that no one could enter the king's court without being summoned by the king. If one did enter uninvited, the king could either accept them in by holding out his scepter or he could have the person executed.

7. Why did Esther want the Jews to fast for three days? (v. 16)

The decree was issued on the thirteenth day of the first month of the year. A three day fast would have meant that the fast occurred during the days of the Passover. How could Esther and her people celebrate their liberation from slavery in Egypt when they were facing annihilation at the hands of the Persians. During their three days fast, they were supposed to offer prayer to the LORD that He would forgive them for their sins and remember that it was the Passover that cemented Israel to the LORD as His people.

Biblical Personalities

1. Hathach – a messenger sent from Esther to speak with Mordecai.

---

[51] Osher Chaim. Levene and Ḥarṭman Yehoshuʻa Daṿid ben Yeḥezḳel., *Jewish Wisdom in the Numbers* (Brooklyn, NY: Mesorah, 2013).

Culture

Discussion

The ordinance of entrance into the presence of the King was enacted to protect the King's life from usurpers and rivals. Kings in the Middle East were assassinated by their wives, sons, and other relatives. Jealousy would occur between wives in large harems and would create hatred for the King, which could lead to assassinations. The King had many concubines and wives as well as servants who might have wanted to kill him.[52]

Questioning the Passage

1. What does "for such a time as this" mean? (v. 14)

   This phrase means "you have come to the kingdom for this cause." Esther was an orphan who rose to become the queen of the Empire. The LORD did this for a reason, and that reason was that Esther was the savior of the Jewish nation. She saved her people from the genocide.[53]

Thoughts

The infraction by the Hebrew people which caused the potential annihilation, was not known to them at first. If the LORD would have sent a messenger to Esther or Mordecai before the seven-day feast of the King, they would have stayed away from the feast. There must have been several violations of the LORD's Law at the feast. Indeed, nonkosher food would have been served. Other physical acts could have occurred that would have been against the LORD's Law. As citizens of Persia and living in Susa they did not have a choice but to participate. The LORD wrote

---

[52] Rocco A. Errico and George M. Lamsa, *Aramaic Light on Ezra through the Song of Solomon* (Smyma, GA: Noohra Foundation, 2010).
[53] IBID.

redemption and salvation into the fabric of the Universe. The LORD knew that even His people would have to sin from time to time in order to survive. This was one of those times. The people fasted for the three days which was on the day of Passover thus demonstrating to the LORD outwardly their inwardly cry for restoration and forgiveness.

Chapter Five

Language

New American Standard 1995	Hebrew
[1] Now it came about on the third day that Esther put on her royal robes and stood in the inner court of the king's palace in front of the king's rooms, and the king was sitting on his royal throne in the throne room, opposite the entrance to the palace. [2] When the king saw Esther the queen standing in the court, she obtained favor in his sight; and the king extended to Esther the golden scepter which *was* in his hand. So Esther came near and touched the top of the scepter. [3] Then the king said to her, "What is *troubling* you, Queen Esther? And what is your request? Even to half of the kingdom it shall be given to you." [4] Esther said, "If it pleases the king, may the king and Haman come this day to the banquet that I have prepared for him." [5] Then the king said, "Bring Haman quickly that we may do as Esther desires." So the king and Haman came to the banquet which Esther had prepared. [6] As they drank their wine at the banquet, the king said to Esther, "What is your petition, for it shall be granted to you. And what is your request? Even to half of the kingdom it shall be done." [7] So Esther replied, "My petition and my request is: [8] if I have found favor in the sight of the king, and if it pleases the king to grant my	וַיְהִ֣י ׀ בַּיֹּ֣ום הַשְּׁלִישִׁ֗י וַתִּלְבַּ֤שׁ אֶסְתֵּר֙ מַלְכ֔וּת וַֽתַּעֲמֹ֞ד בַּחֲצַ֣ר בֵּית־הַמֶּ֗לֶךְ הַפְּנִימִ֔ית נֹ֗כַח בֵּ֣ית הַמֶּ֑לֶךְ וְהַמֶּ֗לֶךְ יֹושֵׁ֞ב עַל־כִּסֵּ֤א מַלְכוּתֹו֙ בְּבֵ֣ית הַמַּלְכ֔וּת נֹ֖כַח פֶּ֥תַח הַבָּֽיִת׃ [2] וַיְהִי֩ כִרְאֹ֨ות הַמֶּ֜לֶךְ אֶת־אֶסְתֵּ֣ר הַמַּלְכָּ֗ה עֹמֶ֙דֶת֙ בֶּֽחָצֵ֔ר נָשְׂאָ֥ה חֵ֖ן בְּעֵינָ֑יו וַיֹּ֨ושֶׁט הַמֶּ֜לֶךְ לְאֶסְתֵּ֗ר אֶת־שַׁרְבִ֤יט הַזָּהָב֙ אֲשֶׁ֣ר בְּיָדֹ֔ו וַתִּקְרַ֣ב אֶסְתֵּ֔ר וַתִּגַּ֖ע בְּרֹ֥אשׁ הַשַּׁרְבִֽיט׃ ס [3] וַיֹּ֤אמֶר לָהּ֙ הַמֶּ֔לֶךְ מַה־לָּ֖ךְ אֶסְתֵּ֣ר הַמַּלְכָּ֑ה וּמַה־בַּקָּשָׁתֵ֛ךְ עַד־חֲצִ֥י הַמַּלְכ֖וּת וְיִנָּ֥תֵֽן לָֽךְ׃ [4] וַתֹּ֣אמֶר אֶסְתֵּ֔ר אִם־עַל־הַמֶּ֖לֶךְ טֹ֑וב יָבֹ֨וא הַמֶּ֤לֶךְ וְהָמָן֙ הַיֹּ֔ום אֶל־הַמִּשְׁתֶּ֖ה אֲשֶׁר־עָשִׂ֥יתִי לֹֽו׃ [5] וַיֹּ֣אמֶר הַמֶּ֗לֶךְ מַהֲרוּ֙ אֶת־הָמָ֔ן לַעֲשֹׂ֖ות אֶת־דְּבַ֣ר אֶסְתֵּ֑ר וַיָּבֹ֤א הַמֶּ֙לֶךְ֙ וְהָמָ֔ן אֶל־הַמִּשְׁתֶּ֖ה אֲשֶׁר־עָשְׂתָ֥ה אֶסְתֵּֽר׃ [6] וַיֹּ֨אמֶר הַמֶּ֤לֶךְ לְאֶסְתֵּר֙ בְּמִשְׁתֵּ֣ה הַיַּ֔יִן מַה־שְּׁאֵלָתֵ֖ךְ וְיִנָּ֣תֵֽן לָ֑ךְ וּמַה־בַּקָּשָׁתֵ֛ךְ עַד־חֲצִ֥י הַמַּלְכ֖וּת וְתֵעָֽשׂ׃ [7] וַתַּ֥עַן אֶסְתֵּ֖ר וַתֹּאמַ֑ר שְׁאֵלָתִ֖י וּבַקָּשָׁתִֽי׃ [8] אִם־מָצָ֨אתִי חֵ֜ן בְּעֵינֵ֣י הַמֶּ֗לֶךְ וְאִם־עַל־הַמֶּ֙לֶךְ֙ טֹ֔וב לָתֵת֙ אֶת־שְׁאֵ֣לָתִ֔י וְלַעֲשֹׂ֖ות אֶת־בַּקָּשָׁתִ֑י יָבֹ֧וא הַמֶּ֣לֶךְ וְהָמָ֗ן אֶל־הַמִּשְׁתֶּה֙ אֲשֶׁ֣ר אֶֽעֱשֶׂ֣ה לָהֶ֔ם וּמָחָ֥ר אֶֽעֱשֶׂ֖ה כִּדְבַ֥ר הַמֶּֽלֶךְ׃ [9] וַיֵּצֵ֤א הָמָן֙ בַּיֹּ֣ום הַה֔וּא שָׂמֵ֖חַ וְטֹ֣וב לֵ֑ב וְכִרְאֹות֩ הָמָ֨ן אֶֽת־מָרְדֳּכַ֜י בְּשַׁ֣עַר הַמֶּ֗לֶךְ וְלֹא־קָם֙ וְלֹא־זָ֣ע מִמֶּ֔נּוּ וַיִּמָּלֵ֥א הָמָ֛ן עַֽל־מָרְדֳּכַ֖י חֵמָֽה׃ [10] וַיִּתְאַפַּ֣ק הָמָ֔ן וַיָּבֹ֖וא אֶל־בֵּיתֹ֑ו וַיִּשְׁלַ֛ח וַיָּבֵ֥א אֶת־אֹהֲבָ֖יו וְאֶת־זֶ֥רֶשׁ אִשְׁתֹּֽו׃

petition and do what I request, may the king and Haman come to the banquet which I will prepare for them, and tomorrow I will do as the king says."

9 Then Haman went out that day glad and pleased of heart; but when Haman saw Mordecai in the king's gate and that he did not stand up or tremble before him, Haman was filled with anger against Mordecai.

10 Haman controlled himself, however, went to his house and sent for his friends and his wife Zeresh.

11 Then Haman recounted to them the glory of his riches, and the number of his sons, and every *instance* where the king had magnified him and how he had promoted him above the princes and servants of the king.

12 Haman also said, "Even Esther the queen let no one but me come with the king to the banquet which she had prepared; and tomorrow also I am invited by her with the king.

13 "Yet all of this does not satisfy me every time I see Mordecai the Jew sitting at the king's gate."

14 Then Zeresh his wife and all his friends said to him, "Have a gallows fifty cubits high made and in the morning ask the king to have Mordecai hanged on it; then go joyfully with the king to the banquet." And the advice pleased Haman, so he had the gallows made.

11 וַיְסַפֵּר לָהֶם הָמָן אֶת־כְּבוֹד עָשְׁרוֹ וְרֹב בָּנָיו וְאֵת כָּל־אֲשֶׁר גִּדְּלוֹ הַמֶּלֶךְ וְאֵת אֲשֶׁר נִשְּׂאוֹ עַל־הַשָּׂרִים וְעַבְדֵי הַמֶּלֶךְ׃

12 וַיֹּאמֶר הָמָן אַף לֹא־הֵבִיאָה אֶסְתֵּר הַמַּלְכָּה עִם־הַמֶּלֶךְ אֶל־הַמִּשְׁתֶּה אֲשֶׁר־עָשָׂתָה כִּי אִם־אוֹתִי וְגַם־לְמָחָר אֲנִי קָרוּא־לָהּ עִם־הַמֶּלֶךְ׃

13 וְכָל־זֶה אֵינֶנּוּ שֹׁוֶה לִי בְּכָל־עֵת אֲשֶׁר אֲנִי רֹאֶה אֶת־מָרְדֳּכַי הַיְּהוּדִי יוֹשֵׁב בְּשַׁעַר הַמֶּלֶךְ׃

14 וַתֹּאמֶר לוֹ זֶרֶשׁ אִשְׁתּוֹ וְכָל־אֹהֲבָיו יַעֲשׂוּ־עֵץ גָּבֹהַּ חֲמִשִּׁים אַמָּה וּבַבֹּקֶר אֱמֹר לַמֶּלֶךְ וְיִתְלוּ אֶת־מָרְדֳּכַי עָלָיו וּבֹא־עִם־הַמֶּלֶךְ אֶל־הַמִּשְׁתֶּה שָׂמֵחַ וַיִּיטַב הַדָּבָר לִפְנֵי הָמָן וַיַּעַשׂ הָעֵץ׃ פ

Process of Discovery

Linguistics Section

Linguistic Structure

A [1] Now it came about on the third day that Esther put on her royal robes and stood in the inner court of the king's palace in front of the king's rooms, and the king was sitting on his royal throne in the throne room, opposite the entrance to the palace. [2] When the king saw Esther the queen standing in the court, she obtained favor in his sight; and the king extended to Esther the golden scepter which *was* in his hand. So Esther came near and touched the top of the scepter.

> **B** [3] Then the king said to her, "What is *troubling* you, Queen Esther? And what is your request? Even to half of the kingdom it shall be given to you." [4] Esther said, "If it pleases the king, may the king and Haman come this day to the banquet that I have prepared for him." [5] Then the king said, "Bring Haman quickly that we may do as Esther desires." So the king and Haman came to the banquet which Esther had prepared. [6] As they drank their wine at the banquet, the king said to Esther, "What is your petition, for it shall be granted to you. And what is your request? Even to half of the kingdom it shall be done." [7] So Esther replied, "My petition and my request is: [8] if I have found favor in the sight of the king, and if it pleases the king to grant my petition and do what I request, may the king and Haman come to the banquet which I will prepare for them, and tomorrow I will do as the king says."

A' [9] Then Haman went out that day glad and pleased of heart; but when Haman saw Mordecai in the king's gate and that he did not stand up or tremble before him, Haman was filled with anger against Mordecai.

> **B'** [10] Haman controlled himself, however, went to his house and sent for his friends and his wife Zeresh. [11] Then Haman recounted to them the glory of his riches, and the number of his sons, and every *instance* where the king had magnified him and how he had promoted him above the princes and servants of the king. [12] Haman also said, "Even Esther the queen let no one but me come with the king to the banquet which she had prepared; and tomorrow also I am

invited by her with the king. [13] "Yet all of this does not satisfy me every time I see Mordecai the Jew sitting at the king's gate."

[14] Then Zeresh his wife and all his friends said to him, "Have a gallows fifty cubits high made and in the morning ask the king to have Mordecai hanged on it; then go joyfully with the king to the banquet." And the advice pleased Haman, so he had the gallows made. (Est. 5:1-14 NAU)

Discussion

This chapter is a simple A-B-A'-B' chiasm. It is formed by Queen Esther holding two banquets for the King.

Questioning the Passage

1. Is there a significance to Esther's three days fast? (v. 1)

   According to the Targum Sheni, verse one includes Esther's prayer to the LORD. In that prayer, she said that she fasted three days in correspondence to the three days it took Abraham to go to Zion to tie up Isaac on the altar before the LORD. Also, she fasted three days corresponding to the three days that Israel stood at the foot of Mount Sinai, waiting for the LORD to speak to the people and for them to accept the Torah.[54]

2. Why did Esther prepare two banquets for the King? (v. 8)

   The Targum Sheni says that Esther held two feasts for the King to soften him up for her request to prevent Haman's order of executing all the Jews in the Empire. She also thought that she could uncover Haman's hatred of the Jews in the presence of the King. The feasts were wine feasts. Therefore, the participants in the feast, especially the King and Haman, actually the only participates, would get drunk. If Esther could get Haman drunk, she could get him to express his

---

[54] "The Aramaic Bible, the Two Targums of Esther" The Liturgical Press. 1991

hatred of the Jews. The second feast occurred because Haman's lips were not loosened and he did not admit his hatred of the Jews. Therefore, a second feast was needed. Unfortunately, the second feast did not result in Haman's confession.[55]

Biblical Personalities

1. Zeresh – she was Haman's wife. According to the Targum Rishon, she was the daughter of Tattenai, the governor of the province, which was on the other side of the river from Susa. The Targum Rishon notes say that Haman had 208 children. Therefore, Haman had to have many wives. Calling Zeresh says that Haman valued her opinion more than any other of his wives. Tattanei is mentioned in Ezra 5:3, 6:6, and 6:13.

Culture Section

Discussion

Questioning the passage

1. What does "half of the kingdom" mean? (v. 3)

   This phrase is an idiom that means the same as "the sky is the limit" today. The King was not going to give Esther half of his kingdom. He did promise to give her whatever she wanted.[56]

---

[55] IBID.

[56] Rocco A. Errico and George M. Lamsa, *Aramaic Light on Ezra through the Song of Solomon* (Smyma, GA: Noohra Foundation, 2010).

2. Why did Haman attempt to kill Mordecai by hanging him in a tree (crucifixion)? (v. 14)

The Targum Rishon says that Haman discussed killing Mordecai with his wife Zeresh and his friends. They told him that if Haman through Mordecai into fire that he would survive like his ancestor Abraham was saved from fire (this is referring to the Midrash that King Nimrod put Abraham into a furnace because he destroyed the idols in his father's idol shop). Haman was told that he could not use a sword because his ancestor Isaac was saved from the sword (when Abraham was about to sacrifice him to the LORD. He was told that he could not use water to suffocate him because Moses' and the Israelites were saved from water when the LORD separated the Red Sea for them. Haman was told that he could not put Mordecai into the lions' den because Daniel was saved from a lions' den. Therefore, Haman had to have Mordecai crucified.[57]

The Targum Sheni adds that Haman could not kill Mordecai by stoning him because David killed Goliath with a stone. He was told that if he had Mordecai cast into bronze that he would extract himself as Manasseh did.[58]

Additional information from the Targum Rishon

In verse one, Esther offers a lengthy prayer to the LORD. In it, she asks the LORD to stop the wickedness of Haman, who was going to have all the Jews in the Empire executed. Esther tells the tale of how Haman caused Vashti's death in the hope that his daughter would become the Queen. To prevent Haman's daughter from becoming the Queen, it was determined by the LORD that she became defiled with excrement and with urine every day after Vashti's death. Therefore, Haman's daughter became

---

[57] "The Aramaic Bible, the Two Targums of Esther" The Liturgical Press. 1991
[58] IBID.

very undesirable to the King. In Esther's prayer, she recaps the genealogy of Haman back to Esau. A conclusion from Esther's prayer is that Haman lashed out at the Jews because his daughter did not become Queen. The reason Haman decided to lash out against the Jews is because of his ancestry.

In verse three, the King offers Esther anything she wanted with one exception. That exception was the rebuilding of the Temple in Jerusalem. The King offered a pledge to Geshem the Arab, to Sanballat the Horonite, and Tobiah the Ammonite slave not to rebuild the temple. The King was concerned that the Jews might revolt if Esther asked for the rebuilding of the Temple in Jerusalem, and he said no. Therefore, she was instructed not to ask for it. Since the King did not know that Esther was a Jew, it is interesting that the Targum Rishon added this commentary. Verse four was Esther's reply and it makes note that Esther told the King that she did not want to request the rebuilding of the Temple. Perhaps this commentary in the Targum indicates that there were non-Jews in the Persian Empire who desired to see the Temple at Jerusalem rebuilt.

In verse nine, the Targum says that Esther established a Sanhedrin for Mordecai and the children of Susa to study the Torah. They met at the gate of the palace. When Haman walked to the gate, he saw the teaching, and when Mordecai did not stand up and bow down to him, Haman became filled with anger.[59]

---

[59] "The Aramaic Bible, the Two Targums of Esther" The Liturgical Press. 1991

Additional information from the Targum Sheni.

In verse two, the Targum Sheni says that Haman was with the King when Esther came to him. Haman was ready to execute Esther immediately. He was very disappointed and upset when the King offered the scepter to Esther.

Thoughts

Esther tried to save her people by not revealing who she was. Instead, she tried to get Haman to admit his hatred to the King. Since the Persian kings favored the LORD, Esther thought that the king would be upset about what Haman did. It might be worth noting that if Esther went in to the king and admitted who she was, the risk to her uncle Mordecai might have been eliminated. Esther was wearing the stranger's face. She was hiding her true identity to the King. She did this for fear of her life because of her deception. However, Mordecai was dragged in. A lesson here is that telling the truth is the best course because the truth always comes forward.

Chapter Six

Language

New American Standard 1995	Hebrew
[1] During that night the king could not sleep so he gave an order to bring the book of records, the chronicles, and they were read before the king. [2] It was found written what Mordecai had reported concerning Bigthana and Teresh, two of the king's eunuchs who were doorkeepers, that they had sought to lay hands on King Ahasuerus. [3] The king said, "What honor or dignity has been bestowed on Mordecai for this?" Then the king's servants who attended him said, "Nothing has been done for him." [4] So the king said, "Who is in the court?" Now Haman had just entered the outer court of the king's palace in order to speak to the king about hanging Mordecai on the gallows which he had prepared for him. [5] The king's servants said to him, "Behold, Haman is standing in the court." And the king said, "Let him come in." [6] So Haman came in and the king said to him, "What is to be done for the man whom the king desires to honor?" And Haman said to himself, "Whom would the king desire to honor more than me?" [7] Then Haman said to the king, "For the man whom the king desires to honor,	בַּלַּיְלָה הַהוּא נָדְדָה שְׁנַת הַמֶּלֶךְ וַיֹּאמֶר לְהָבִיא אֶת־סֵפֶר הַזִּכְרֹנוֹת דִּבְרֵי הַיָּמִים וַיִּהְיוּ נִקְרָאִים לִפְנֵי הַמֶּלֶךְ: [2] וַיִּמָּצֵא כָתוּב אֲשֶׁר הִגִּיד מָרְדֳּכַי עַל־בִּגְתָנָא וָתֶרֶשׁ שְׁנֵי סָרִיסֵי הַמֶּלֶךְ מִשֹּׁמְרֵי הַסַּף אֲשֶׁר בִּקְשׁוּ לִשְׁלֹחַ יָד בַּמֶּלֶךְ אֲחַשְׁוֵרוֹשׁ: [3] וַיֹּאמֶר הַמֶּלֶךְ מַה־נַּעֲשָׂה יְקָר וּגְדוּלָּה לְמָרְדֳּכַי עַל־זֶה וַיֹּאמְרוּ נַעֲרֵי הַמֶּלֶךְ מְשָׁרְתָיו לֹא־נַעֲשָׂה עִמּוֹ דָּבָר: [4] וַיֹּאמֶר הַמֶּלֶךְ מִי בֶחָצֵר וְהָמָן בָּא לַחֲצַר בֵּית־הַמֶּלֶךְ הַחִיצוֹנָה לֵאמֹר לַמֶּלֶךְ לִתְלוֹת אֶת־מָרְדֳּכַי עַל־הָעֵץ אֲשֶׁר־הֵכִין לוֹ: [5] וַיֹּאמְרוּ נַעֲרֵי הַמֶּלֶךְ אֵלָיו הִנֵּה הָמָן עֹמֵד בֶּחָצֵר וַיֹּאמֶר הַמֶּלֶךְ יָבוֹא: [6] וַיָּבוֹא הָמָן וַיֹּאמֶר לוֹ הַמֶּלֶךְ מַה־לַעֲשׂוֹת בָּאִישׁ אֲשֶׁר הַמֶּלֶךְ חָפֵץ בִּיקָרוֹ וַיֹּאמֶר הָמָן בְּלִבּוֹ לְמִי יַחְפֹּץ הַמֶּלֶךְ לַעֲשׂוֹת יְקָר יוֹתֵר מִמֶּנִּי: [7] וַיֹּאמֶר הָמָן אֶל־הַמֶּלֶךְ אִישׁ אֲשֶׁר הַמֶּלֶךְ חָפֵץ בִּיקָרוֹ: [8] יָבִיאוּ לְבוּשׁ מַלְכוּת אֲשֶׁר לָבַשׁ־בּוֹ הַמֶּלֶךְ וְסוּס אֲשֶׁר רָכַב עָלָיו הַמֶּלֶךְ וַאֲשֶׁר נִתַּן כֶּתֶר מַלְכוּת בְּרֹאשׁוֹ: [9] וְנָתוֹן הַלְּבוּשׁ וְהַסּוּס עַל־יַד־אִישׁ מִשָּׂרֵי הַמֶּלֶךְ הַפַּרְתְּמִים וְהִלְבִּישׁוּ אֶת־הָאִישׁ אֲשֶׁר הַמֶּלֶךְ חָפֵץ בִּיקָרוֹ וְהִרְכִּיבֻהוּ עַל־הַסּוּס בִּרְחוֹב הָעִיר וְקָרְאוּ לְפָנָיו כָּכָה יֵעָשֶׂה לָאִישׁ אֲשֶׁר הַמֶּלֶךְ חָפֵץ בִּיקָרוֹ: [10] וַיֹּאמֶר הַמֶּלֶךְ לְהָמָן מַהֵר קַח אֶת־הַלְּבוּשׁ וְאֶת־הַסּוּס כַּאֲשֶׁר דִּבַּרְתָּ וַעֲשֵׂה־כֵן לְמָרְדֳּכַי

⁸ let them bring a royal robe which the king has worn, and the horse on which the king has ridden, and on whose head a royal crown has been placed;

⁹ and let the robe and the horse be handed over to one of the king's most noble princes and let them array the man whom the king desires to honor and lead him on horseback through the city square, and proclaim before him, 'Thus it shall be done to the man whom the king desires to honor.'"

¹⁰ Then the king said to Haman, "Take quickly the robes and the horse as you have said, and do so for Mordecai the Jew, who is sitting at the king's gate; do not fall short in anything of all that you have said."

¹¹ So Haman took the robe and the horse, and arrayed Mordecai, and led him *on horseback* through the city square, and proclaimed before him, "Thus it shall be done to the man whom the king desires to honor."

¹² Then Mordecai returned to the king's gate. But Haman hurried home, mourning, with *his* head covered.

¹³ Haman recounted to Zeresh his wife and all his friends everything that had happened to him. Then his wise men and Zeresh his wife said to him, "If Mordecai, before whom you have begun to fall, is of Jewish origin, you will not overcome him, but will surely fall before him."

¹⁴ While they were still talking with him, the king's eunuchs arrived and hastily brought Haman to the banquet which Esther had prepared.

הַיְּהוּדִי הַיּוֹשֵׁב בְּשַׁעַר הַמֶּלֶךְ אַל־תַּפֵּל דָּבָר מִכֹּל אֲשֶׁר דִּבַּרְתָּ:

¹¹ וַיִּקַּח הָמָן אֶת־הַלְּבוּשׁ וְאֶת־הַסּוּס וַיַּלְבֵּשׁ אֶת־מָרְדֳּכָי וַיַּרְכִּיבֵהוּ בִּרְחוֹב הָעִיר וַיִּקְרָא לְפָנָיו כָּכָה יֵעָשֶׂה לָאִישׁ אֲשֶׁר הַמֶּלֶךְ חָפֵץ בִּיקָרוֹ:

¹² וַיָּשָׁב מָרְדֳּכַי אֶל־שַׁעַר הַמֶּלֶךְ וְהָמָן נִדְחַף אֶל־בֵּיתוֹ אָבֵל וַחֲפוּי רֹאשׁ:

¹³ וַיְסַפֵּר הָמָן לְזֶרֶשׁ אִשְׁתּוֹ וּלְכָל־אֹהֲבָיו אֵת כָּל־אֲשֶׁר קָרָהוּ וַיֹּאמְרוּ לוֹ חֲכָמָיו וְזֶרֶשׁ אִשְׁתּוֹ אִם מִזֶּרַע הַיְּהוּדִים מָרְדֳּכַי אֲשֶׁר הַחִלּוֹתָ לִנְפֹּל לְפָנָיו לֹא־תוּכַל לוֹ כִּי־נָפוֹל תִּפּוֹל לְפָנָיו:

¹⁴ עוֹדָם מְדַבְּרִים עִמּוֹ וְסָרִיסֵי הַמֶּלֶךְ הִגִּיעוּ וַיַּבְהִלוּ לְהָבִיא אֶת־הָמָן אֶל־הַמִּשְׁתֶּה אֲשֶׁר־עָשְׂתָה אֶסְתֵּר:

Process of Discovery

Linguistics Section

Linguistic Structure

A [1] During that night the king could not sleep so he gave an order to bring the book of records, the chronicles, and they were read before the king. [2] It was found written what Mordecai had reported concerning Bigthana and Teresh, two of the king's eunuchs who were doorkeepers, that they had sought to lay hands on King Ahasuerus. [3] The king said, "What honor or dignity has been bestowed on Mordecai for this?" Then the king's servants who attended him said, "Nothing has been done for him."

B [4] So the king said, "Who is in the court?" Now Haman had just entered the outer court of the king's palace in order to speak to the king about hanging Mordecai on the gallows which he had prepared for him. [5] The king's servants said to him, "Behold, Haman is standing in the court." And the king said, "Let him come in."

C [6] So Haman came in and the king said to him, "What is to be done for the man whom the king desires to honor?" And Haman said to himself, "Whom would the king desire to honor more than me?"

D [7] Then Haman said to the king, "For the man whom the king desires to honor, [8] let them bring a royal robe which the king has worn, and the horse on which the king has ridden, and on whose head a royal crown has been placed; [9] and let the robe and the horse be handed over to one of the king's most noble princes and let them array the man whom the king desires to honor and lead him on horseback through the city square, and proclaim before him, 'Thus it shall be done to the man whom the king desires to honor.'"

C' [10] Then the king said to Haman, "Take quickly the robes and the horse as you have said, and do so for Mordecai the Jew, who is sitting at the king's gate; do not fall short in anything of all that you have said."

B' [11] So Haman took the robe and the horse, and arrayed Mordecai, and led him *on horseback* through the city square, and proclaimed before him, "Thus it shall be done to the man whom the king desires to honor." [12] Then Mordecai returned to the king's gate. But Haman hurried home, mourning, with *his* head covered. [13] Haman recounted to Zeresh his wife and all his friends everything that had happened to him. Then his wise men and Zeresh his wife said to him, "If Mordecai, before whom you have begun to fall, is of Jewish origin, you will not overcome him, but will surely fall before him."

A' [14] While they were still talking with him, the king's eunuchs arrived and hastily brought Haman to the banquet which Esther had prepared.

Discussion

Haman goes to ask King Ahasuerus to kill Mordecai for not bowing to him and instead of the King forces Haman to honor Mordecai. The center of the chiasm is how Haman was to honor Mordecai.

Questioning the Passage

1. Why could not the king sleep? (v. 1)

   According to the Targum Rishon, the angels heard a cry from the Earth. They first thought it was the voices of young goats. They came before the LORD to tell the LORD about the voices. The LORD said to them that the voices were from the women of Israel crying out to the LORD because of what Haman was going to have done to them. The LORD decided to send the angel of disturbance to the King so that he could not sleep that night. In the middle of the night, the King ordered his scribe to bring the book of the chronicles to him.[60]

---

[60] "The Aramaic Bible, the Two Targums of Esther" The Liturgical Press. 1991

The Targum Sheni says that the night the king could not sleep was the night that Sarah was taken to the house of Abimelek. It is also the night when the firstborn of Egypt was slain.[61]

Additional Information from the Targums

In verse 11, Haman was leading the horse which Mordecai was sitting on. When Haman passed by his house, his daughter Shlakhtevath looked down and thought that the man on the horse was her father. She took a pot of excrement and threw some on the head of Haman (who was walking in front of the horse). Haman looked at his daughter and said: "You, too, my daughter, you embarrass me." His daughter fell from the roof and died from the balcony chamber.[62]

Thoughts

Haman thought that he was to be honored then learned that it was Mordecai who was honored. It is an echo of why Yeshua said that when one goes to a banquet, it is better to sit in the least essential seat and be moved to a better seat by the host of the banquet.

---

[61] IBID.
[62] IBID.

Chapter Seven

Language

New American Standard 1995	Hebrew
[1] Now the king and Haman came to drink *wine* with Esther the queen.	וַיָּבֹא הַמֶּלֶךְ וְהָמָן לִשְׁתּוֹת עִם־אֶסְתֵּר הַמַּלְכָּה׃ [2] וַיֹּאמֶר הַמֶּלֶךְ לְאֶסְתֵּר גַּם בַּיּוֹם הַשֵּׁנִי בְּמִשְׁתֵּה הַיַּיִן מַה־שְּׁאֵלָתֵךְ אֶסְתֵּר הַמַּלְכָּה וְתִנָּתֵן לָךְ וּמַה־בַּקָּשָׁתֵךְ עַד־חֲצִי הַמַּלְכוּת וְתֵעָשׂ׃
[2] And the king said to Esther on the second day also as they drank their wine at the banquet, "What is your petition, Queen Esther? It shall be granted you. And what is your request? Even to half of the kingdom it shall be done."	[3] וַתַּעַן אֶסְתֵּר הַמַּלְכָּה וַתֹּאמַר אִם־מָצָאתִי חֵן בְּעֵינֶיךָ הַמֶּלֶךְ וְאִם־עַל־הַמֶּלֶךְ טוֹב תִּנָּתֶן־לִי נַפְשִׁי בִּשְׁאֵלָתִי וְעַמִּי בְּבַקָּשָׁתִי׃
[3] Then Queen Esther replied, "If I have found favor in your sight, O king, and if it pleases the king, let my life be given me as my petition, and my people as my request;	[4] כִּי נִמְכַּרְנוּ אֲנִי וְעַמִּי לְהַשְׁמִיד לַהֲרוֹג וּלְאַבֵּד וְאִלּוּ לַעֲבָדִים וְלִשְׁפָחוֹת נִמְכַּרְנוּ הֶחֱרַשְׁתִּי כִּי אֵין הַצָּר שֹׁוֶה בְּנֵזֶק הַמֶּלֶךְ׃ ס
[4] for we have been sold, I and my people, to be destroyed, to be killed and to be annihilated. Now if we had only been sold as slaves, men and women, I would have remained silent, for the trouble would not be commensurate with the annoyance to the king."	[5] וַיֹּאמֶר הַמֶּלֶךְ אֲחַשְׁוֵרוֹשׁ וַיֹּאמֶר לְאֶסְתֵּר הַמַּלְכָּה מִי הוּא זֶה וְאֵי־זֶה הוּא אֲשֶׁר־מְלָאוֹ לִבּוֹ לַעֲשׂוֹת כֵּן׃
[5] Then King Ahasuerus asked Queen Esther, "Who is he, and where is he, who would presume to do thus?"	[6] וַתֹּאמֶר אֶסְתֵּר אִישׁ צַר וְאוֹיֵב הָמָן הָרָע הַזֶּה וְהָמָן נִבְעַת מִלִּפְנֵי הַמֶּלֶךְ וְהַמַּלְכָּה׃
[6] Esther said, "A foe and an enemy is this wicked Haman!" Then Haman became terrified before the king and queen.	[7] וְהַמֶּלֶךְ קָם בַּחֲמָתוֹ מִמִּשְׁתֵּה הַיַּיִן אֶל־גִּנַּת הַבִּיתָן וְהָמָן עָמַד לְבַקֵּשׁ עַל־נַפְשׁוֹ מֵאֶסְתֵּר הַמַּלְכָּה כִּי רָאָה כִּי־כָלְתָה אֵלָיו הָרָעָה מֵאֵת הַמֶּלֶךְ׃
[7] The king arose in his anger from drinking wine *and went* into the palace garden; but Haman stayed to beg for his life from Queen Esther, for he saw that harm had been determined against him by the king.	[8] וְהַמֶּלֶךְ שָׁב מִגִּנַּת הַבִּיתָן אֶל־בֵּית מִשְׁתֵּה הַיַּיִן וְהָמָן נֹפֵל עַל־הַמִּטָּה אֲשֶׁר אֶסְתֵּר עָלֶיהָ וַיֹּאמֶר הַמֶּלֶךְ הֲגַם לִכְבּוֹשׁ אֶת־הַמַּלְכָּה עִמִּי בַּבָּיִת הַדָּבָר יָצָא מִפִּי הַמֶּלֶךְ וּפְנֵי הָמָן חָפוּ׃ ס
	[9] וַיֹּאמֶר חַרְבוֹנָה אֶחָד מִן־הַסָּרִיסִים לִפְנֵי הַמֶּלֶךְ גַּם הִנֵּה־הָעֵץ אֲשֶׁר־עָשָׂה הָמָן לְמָרְדֳּכַי אֲשֶׁר דִּבֶּר־טוֹב עַל־הַמֶּלֶךְ עֹמֵד בְּבֵית הָמָן גָּבֹהַּ חֲמִשִּׁים אַמָּה וַיֹּאמֶר הַמֶּלֶךְ תְּלֻהוּ עָלָיו׃
	[10] וַיִּתְלוּ אֶת־הָמָן עַל־הָעֵץ אֲשֶׁר־הֵכִין לְמָרְדֳּכָי וַחֲמַת הַמֶּלֶךְ שָׁכָכָה׃ פ

[8] Now when the king returned from the palace garden into the place where they were drinking wine, Haman was falling on the couch where Esther was. Then the king said, "Will he even assault the queen with me in the house?" As the word went out of the king's mouth, they covered Haman's face.

[9] Then Harbonah, one of the eunuchs who *were* before the king said, "Behold indeed, the gallows standing at Haman's house fifty cubits high, which Haman made for Mordecai who spoke good on behalf of the king!" And the king said, "Hang him on it."

[10] So they hanged Haman on the gallows which he had prepared for Mordecai, and the king's anger subsided.

Process of Discovery

Linguistics Section

Linguistic Structure

[Transition to the banquet] [1] Now the king and Haman came to drink *wine* with Esther the queen. [2] And the king said to Esther on the second day also as they drank their wine at the banquet, "What is your petition, Queen Esther? It shall be granted you. And what is your request? Even to half of the kingdom it shall be done."

A [Esther's request] [3] Then Queen Esther replied, "If I have found favor in your sight, O king, and if it pleases the king, let my life be given me as my petition, and my people as my request; [4] for we have been sold, I and my people, to be destroyed, to be killed and to be annihilated. Now if we had only been sold as slaves, men and women, I would have remained silent, for the trouble would not be commensurate with the annoyance to the king."

> **B [Ahasuerus' reply]** [5] Then King Ahasuerus asked Queen Esther, "Who is he, and where is he, who would presume to do thus?" [6] Esther said, "A foe and an enemy is this wicked Haman!" Then Haman became terrified before the king and queen.

A' [The King leaves Esther alone with Haman] [7] The king arose in his anger from drinking wine *and went* into the palace garden; but Haman stayed to beg for his life from Queen Esther, for he saw that harm had been determined against him by the king.

> **B' [The King returns]** [8] Now when the king returned from the palace garden into the place where they were drinking wine, Haman was falling on the couch where Esther was. Then the king said, "Will he even assault the queen with me in the house?" As the word went out of the king's mouth, they covered Haman's face.

[The decree] [9] Then Harbonah, one of the eunuchs who *were* before the king said, "Behold indeed, the gallows standing at Haman's house fifty cubits high, which Haman made for Mordecai who spoke good on behalf of the king!" And the king said, "Hang him on it." [10] So they hanged Haman on the gallows which he had prepared for Mordecai, and the king's anger subsided.

Discussion

The second wine feast did not loosen Haman's tongue. Therefore, Esther had no choice but to take the risk of revealing her heritage to the King. Haman was then executed for his wickedness on the cross that he constructed for Mordecai.

Questioning the Passage

1. What does it mean "for we have been sold in verse 4?

    This is a reference to chapter three, verse nine.

Biblical Personalities

1. Harbonah – a eunuch of the King

Additional information from the Targums

Verse seven, the Targum Rishon says that the King raised his eyes and saw ten angels resembling the ten sons of Haman who were cutting down trees from the inner garden. Later in the Esther story, Haman's ten sons were killed. Since ten represents perfection, the LORD needed to show the King that Haman was not perfection. The killing of his ten sons demonstrated the evil in Haman, who posed as good.[63]

Thoughts

Not only did Haman lose his life, but he sacrificed his ten sons. The number ten reminds us that evil can manifest itself in our world and look like perfection. Perfection in evil is difficult to see. When it is missed, evil can run wild. Keeping faith in the works of the LORD allowed Esther to have the courage to save her people and

---

[63] "The Aramaic Bible, the Two Targums of Esther" The Liturgical Press. 1991

to expose the treachery of Haman. The King repaid Haman's evil with the death of his sons. The LORD gave the King this vision when he went into the garden for a few minutes.

Chapter Eight

Language

New American Standard 1995	Hebrew
[1] On that day King Ahasuerus gave the house of Haman, the enemy of the Jews, to Queen Esther; and Mordecai came before the king, for Esther had disclosed what he was to her.	בַּיּוֹם הַהוּא נָתַן הַמֶּלֶךְ אֲחַשְׁוֵרוֹשׁ לְאֶסְתֵּר הַמַּלְכָּה אֶת־בֵּית הָמָן צֹרֵר (הַיְּהוּדִיִּים) [הַיְּהוּדִים] וּמָרְדֳּכַי בָּא לִפְנֵי הַמֶּלֶךְ כִּי־הִגִּידָה אֶסְתֵּר מַה הוּא־לָהּ׃
[2] The king took off his signet ring which he had taken away from Haman, and gave it to Mordecai. And Esther set Mordecai over the house of Haman.	וַיָּסַר הַמֶּלֶךְ אֶת־טַבַּעְתּוֹ אֲשֶׁר הֶעֱבִיר מֵהָמָן וַיִּתְּנָהּ לְמָרְדֳּכָי וַתָּשֶׂם אֶסְתֵּר אֶת־מָרְדֳּכַי עַל־בֵּית הָמָן׃ פ
[3] Then Esther spoke again to the king, fell at his feet, wept and implored him to avert the evil *scheme* of Haman the Agagite and his plot which he had devised against the Jews.	וַתּוֹסֶף אֶסְתֵּר וַתְּדַבֵּר לִפְנֵי הַמֶּלֶךְ וַתִּפֹּל לִפְנֵי רַגְלָיו וַתֵּבְךְּ וַתִּתְחַנֶּן־לוֹ לְהַעֲבִיר אֶת־רָעַת הָמָן הָאֲגָגִי וְאֵת מַחֲשַׁבְתּוֹ אֲשֶׁר חָשַׁב עַל־הַיְּהוּדִים׃
[4] The king extended the golden scepter to Esther. So Esther arose and stood before the king.	וַיּוֹשֶׁט הַמֶּלֶךְ לְאֶסְתֵּר אֵת שַׁרְבִט הַזָּהָב וַתָּקָם אֶסְתֵּר וַתַּעֲמֹד לִפְנֵי הַמֶּלֶךְ׃
[5] Then she said, "If it pleases the king and if I have found favor before him and the matter *seems* proper to the king and I am pleasing in his sight, let it be written to revoke the letters devised by Haman, the son of Hammedatha the Agagite, which he wrote to destroy the Jews who are in all the king's provinces.	וַתֹּאמֶר אִם־עַל־הַמֶּלֶךְ טוֹב וְאִם־מָצָאתִי חֵן לְפָנָיו וְכָשֵׁר הַדָּבָר לִפְנֵי הַמֶּלֶךְ וְטוֹבָה אֲנִי בְּעֵינָיו יִכָּתֵב לְהָשִׁיב אֶת־הַסְּפָרִים מַחֲשֶׁבֶת הָמָן בֶּן־הַמְּדָתָא הָאֲגָגִי אֲשֶׁר כָּתַב לְאַבֵּד אֶת־הַיְּהוּדִים אֲשֶׁר בְּכָל־מְדִינוֹת הַמֶּלֶךְ׃
[6] "For how can I endure to see the calamity which will befall my people, and how can I endure to see the destruction of my kindred?"	כִּי אֵיכָכָה אוּכַל וְרָאִיתִי בָּרָעָה אֲשֶׁר־יִמְצָא אֶת־עַמִּי וְאֵיכָכָה אוּכַל וְרָאִיתִי בְּאָבְדַן מוֹלַדְתִּי׃ ס
[7] So King Ahasuerus said to Queen Esther and to Mordecai the Jew, "Behold, I have given the house of Haman to Esther, and him they have hanged on the	וַיֹּאמֶר הַמֶּלֶךְ אֲחַשְׁוֵרֹשׁ לְאֶסְתֵּר הַמַּלְכָּה וּלְמָרְדֳּכַי הַיְּהוּדִי הִנֵּה בֵית־הָמָן נָתַתִּי לְאֶסְתֵּר וְאֹתוֹ תָּלוּ עַל־הָעֵץ עַל אֲשֶׁר־שָׁלַח יָדוֹ (בַּיְּהוּדִיִּים) [בַּיְּהוּדִים]׃
	[8] וְאַתֶּם כִּתְבוּ עַל־הַיְּהוּדִים כַּטּוֹב בְּעֵינֵיכֶם בְּשֵׁם הַמֶּלֶךְ וְחִתְמוּ בְּטַבַּעַת הַמֶּלֶךְ כִּי־כְתָב אֲשֶׁר־נִכְתָּב בְּשֵׁם־הַמֶּלֶךְ וְנַחְתּוֹם בְּטַבַּעַת הַמֶּלֶךְ אֵין לְהָשִׁיב׃
	[9] וַיִּקָּרְאוּ סֹפְרֵי־הַמֶּלֶךְ בָּעֵת־הַהִיא בַּחֹדֶשׁ הַשְּׁלִישִׁי הוּא־חֹדֶשׁ סִיוָן בִּשְׁלוֹשָׁה וְעֶשְׂרִים בּוֹ וַיִּכָּתֵב כְּכָל־אֲשֶׁר־צִוָּה מָרְדֳּכַי אֶל־

gallows because he had stretched out his hands against the Jews.

8 "Now you write to the Jews as you see fit, in the king's name, and seal *it* with the king's signet ring; for a decree which is written in the name of the king and sealed with the king's signet ring may not be revoked."

9 So the king's scribes were called at that time in the third month (that is, the month Sivan), on the twenty-third day; and it was written according to all that Mordecai commanded to the Jews, the satraps, the governors and the princes of the provinces which *extended* from India to Ethiopia, 127 provinces, to every province according to its script, and to every people according to their language as well as to the Jews according to their script and their language.

10 He wrote in the name of King Ahasuerus, and sealed it with the king's signet ring, and sent letters by couriers on horses, riding on steeds sired by the royal stud.

11 In them the king granted the Jews who were in each and every city *the right* to assemble and to defend their lives, to destroy, to kill and to annihilate the entire army of any people or province which might attack them, including children and women, and to plunder their spoil,

12 on one day in all the provinces of King Ahasuerus, the thirteenth *day* of the twelfth month (that is, the month Adar).

13 A copy of the edict to be issued as law in each and every province was published to all the peoples, so that the Jews would be ready for this day to avenge themselves on their enemies.

הַיְּהוּדִים וְאֶל הָאֲחַשְׁדַּרְפְּנִים־וְהַפַּחוֹת וְשָׂרֵי
הַמְּדִינוֹת אֲשֶׁר ׀ מֵהֹדּוּ וְעַד־כּוּשׁ שֶׁבַע
וְעֶשְׂרִים וּמֵאָה מְדִינָה מְדִינָה וּמְדִינָה
כִּכְתָבָהּ וְעַם וָעָם כִּלְשֹׁנוֹ וְאֶל־הַיְּהוּדִים
כִּכְתָבָם וְכִלְשׁוֹנָם:

10 וַיִּכְתֹּב בְּשֵׁם הַמֶּלֶךְ אֲחַשְׁוֵרֹשׁ וַיַּחְתֹּם
בְּטַבַּעַת הַמֶּלֶךְ וַיִּשְׁלַח סְפָרִים בְּיַד הָרָצִים
בַּסּוּסִים רֹכְבֵי הָרֶכֶשׁ הָאֲחַשְׁתְּרָנִים בְּנֵי
הָרַמָּכִים:

11 אֲשֶׁר נָתַן הַמֶּלֶךְ לַיְּהוּדִים ׀ אֲשֶׁר בְּכָל־
עִיר־וָעִיר לְהִקָּהֵל וְלַעֲמֹד עַל־נַפְשָׁם
לְהַשְׁמִיד וְלַהֲרֹג וּלְאַבֵּד אֶת־כָּל־חֵיל עַם
וּמְדִינָה הַצָּרִים אֹתָם טַף וְנָשִׁים וּשְׁלָלָם
לָבוֹז:

12 בְּיוֹם אֶחָד בְּכָל־מְדִינוֹת הַמֶּלֶךְ אֲחַשְׁוֵרוֹשׁ
בִּשְׁלוֹשָׁה עָשָׂר לְחֹדֶשׁ שְׁנֵים־עָשָׂר הוּא־
חֹדֶשׁ אֲדָר:

13 פַּתְשֶׁגֶן הַכְּתָב לְהִנָּתֵן דָּת בְּכָל־מְדִינָה
וּמְדִינָה גָּלוּי לְכָל־הָעַמִּים וְלִהְיוֹת
(הַיְּהוּדִיים) [הַיְּהוּדִים] (עתודים) [עֲתִידִים]
לַיּוֹם הַזֶּה לְהִנָּקֵם מֵאֹיְבֵיהֶם:

14 הָרָצִים רֹכְבֵי הָרֶכֶשׁ הָאֲחַשְׁתְּרָנִים יָצְאוּ
מְבֹהָלִים וּדְחוּפִים בִּדְבַר הַמֶּלֶךְ וְהַדָּת נִתְּנָה
בְּשׁוּשַׁן הַבִּירָה: פ

15 וּמָרְדֳּכַי יָצָא ׀ מִלִּפְנֵי הַמֶּלֶךְ בִּלְבוּשׁ מַלְכוּת
תְּכֵלֶת וָחוּר וַעֲטֶרֶת זָהָב גְּדוֹלָה וְתַכְרִיךְ בּוּץ
וְאַרְגָּמָן וְהָעִיר שׁוּשָׁן צָהֲלָה וְשָׂמֵחָה:

16 לַיְּהוּדִים הָיְתָה אוֹרָה וְשִׂמְחָה וְשָׂשֹׂן וִיקָר:

17 וּבְכָל־מְדִינָה וּמְדִינָה וּבְכָל־עִיר וָעִיר
מְקוֹם אֲשֶׁר דְּבַר־הַמֶּלֶךְ וְדָתוֹ מַגִּיעַ שִׂמְחָה
וְשָׂשׂוֹן לַיְּהוּדִים מִשְׁתֶּה וְיוֹם טוֹב וְרַבִּים
מֵעַמֵּי הָאָרֶץ מִתְיַהֲדִים כִּי־נָפַל פַּחַד־
הַיְּהוּדִים עֲלֵיהֶם:

[14] The couriers, hastened and impelled by the king's command, went out, riding on the royal steeds; and the decree was given out at the citadel in Susa.

[15] Then Mordecai went out from the presence of the king in royal robes of blue and white, with a large crown of gold and a garment of fine linen and purple; and the city of Susa shouted and rejoiced.

[16] For the Jews there was light and gladness and joy and honor.

[17] In each and every province and in each and every city, wherever the king's commandment and his decree arrived, there was gladness and joy for the Jews, a feast and a holiday. And many among the peoples of the land became Jews, for the dread of the Jews had fallen on them.

Process of Discovery

Linguistics Section

Linguistic Structure

A [1] On that day King Ahasuerus gave the house of Haman, the enemy of the Jews, to Queen Esther; and Mordecai came before the king, for Esther had disclosed what he was to her. [2] The king took off his signet ring which he had taken away from Haman, and gave it to Mordecai. And Esther set Mordecai over the house of Haman.

> **B** [3] Then Esther spoke again to the king, fell at his feet, wept and implored him to avert the evil *scheme* of Haman the Agagite and his plot which he had devised against the Jews. [4] The king extended the golden scepter to Esther. So Esther arose and stood before the king. [5] Then she said, "If it pleases the king and if I have found favor before him and the matter *seems* proper to the king and I am pleasing in his sight, let it be written to revoke the letters devised by Haman, the son of Hammedatha the Agagite, which he wrote to destroy the Jews who are in all the king's provinces. [6] "For how can I endure to see the calamity which will befall my people, and how can I endure to see the destruction of my kindred?"

A' [7] So King Ahasuerus said to Queen Esther and to Mordecai the Jew, "Behold, I have given the house of Haman to Esther, and him they have hanged on the gallows because he had stretched out his hands against the Jews. [8] "Now you write to the Jews as you see fit, in the king's name, and seal *it* with the king's signet ring; for a decree which is written in the name of the king and sealed with the king's signet ring may not be revoked."

A [9] So the king's scribes were called at that time in the third month (that is, the month Sivan), on the twenty-third day; and it was written according to all that Mordecai commanded to the Jews, the satraps, the governors and the princes of the provinces which *extended* from India to Ethiopia, 127 provinces, to every province according to its script, and to every people according to their language as well as to the Jews according to their script and their language. [10] He wrote in the name of King Ahasuerus, and sealed it with the king's signet ring, and sent letters by couriers on horses, riding on steeds sired by the royal stud.

B [11] In them the king granted the Jews who were in each and every city *the right* to assemble and to defend their lives, to destroy, to kill and to annihilate the entire army of any people or province which might attack them, including children and women, and to plunder their spoil,

> **C** [12] on one day in all the provinces of King Ahasuerus, the thirteenth *day* of the twelfth month (that is, the month Adar).

B' [13] A copy of the edict to be issued as law in each and every province was published to all the peoples, so that the Jews would be ready for this day to avenge themselves on their enemies.

[14] The couriers, hastened and impelled by the king's command, went out, riding on the royal steeds; and the decree was given out at the citadel in Susa. [15] Then Mordecai went out from the presence of the king in royal robes of blue and white, with a large crown of gold and a garment of fine linen and p urple; and the city of Susa shouted and rejoiced. [16] For the Jews there was light and gladness and joy and honor. [17] In each and every province and in each and every city, wherever the king's commandment and his decree arrived, there was gladness and joy for the Jews, a feast and a holiday. And many among the peoples of the land became Jews, for the dread of the Jews had fallen on them.

Discussion

This chapter contains two chiasms. The first one is Queen Esther begging for the Jews in Persia to be saved. The second chiasm is the King's decree for the Jews to save themselves. Verse seventeen refers to the institution of the holiday of Purim.

Thoughts

Esther takes on the challenge from her uncle Mordecai and comes before the King and confesses her heritage and pleads for her people to be saved. The King showed her mercy by extending the septor to her. The King honored Mordecai by giving him the signet ring making Mordecai a powerful man of the Empire. Unfortunately, the King could not rescind a royal decree. So, the King made a new royal decree that the Jews of Persia were to protect themselves on the day that Haman had selected for their execution. In good Jewish fashion, the holiday of Purim is: (1) They tried to kill us; (2) God intervened; (3) Let us eat.

Esther became the savior of her people. What are the dangers today facing the LORD's people? The annihilation of the LORD's people both Jews and Christians in the United States and Western Europe is coming from the culture of society. In the United States, there are groups of atheists who are forcing the government to abandon the building blocks of the government, which is the Holy Bible. Attendance and membership in synagogues and churches are dropping to dangerously low levels. How will future generations learn about the good works of the LORD if there is no one left to tell them about them? The political infighting of these organizations needs to stop. That energy must be spent on telling people about the LORD!

Chapter Nine

Language

New American Standard 1995	Hebrew
¹ Now in the twelfth month (that is, the month Adar), on the thirteenth day when the king's command and edict were about to be executed, on the day when the enemies of the Jews hoped to gain the mastery over them, it was turned to the contrary so that the Jews themselves gained the mastery over those who hated them. ² The Jews assembled in their cities throughout all the provinces of King Ahasuerus to lay hands on those who sought their harm; and no one could stand before them, for the dread of them had fallen on all the peoples. ³ Even all the princes of the provinces, the satraps, the governors and those who were doing the king's business assisted the Jews, because the dread of Mordecai had fallen on them. ⁴ Indeed, Mordecai was great in the king's house, and his fame spread throughout all the provinces; for the man Mordecai became greater and greater. ⁵ Thus the Jews struck all their enemies with the sword, killing and destroying; and they did what they pleased to those who hated them. ⁶ At the citadel in Susa the Jews killed and destroyed five hundred men, ⁷ and Parshandatha, Dalphon, Aspatha, ⁸ Poratha, Adalia, Aridatha, ⁹ Parmashta, Arisai, Aridai and Vaizatha,	וּבִשְׁנֵים עָשָׂר חֹדֶשׁ הוּא־חֹדֶשׁ אֲדָר בִּשְׁלוֹשָׁה עָשָׂר יוֹם בּוֹ אֲשֶׁר הִגִּיעַ דְּבַר־ הַמֶּלֶךְ וְדָתוֹ לְהֵעָשׂוֹת בַּיּוֹם אֲשֶׁר שִׂבְּרוּ אֹיְבֵי הַיְּהוּדִים לִשְׁלוֹט בָּהֶם וְנַהֲפוֹךְ הוּא אֲשֶׁר יִשְׁלְטוּ הַיְּהוּדִים הֵמָּה בְּשֹׂנְאֵיהֶם: ² נִקְהֲלוּ הַיְּהוּדִים בְּעָרֵיהֶם בְּכָל־מְדִינוֹת הַמֶּלֶךְ אֲחַשְׁוֵרוֹשׁ לִשְׁלֹחַ יָד בִּמְבַקְשֵׁי רָעָתָם וְאִישׁ לֹא־עָמַד לִפְנֵיהֶם כִּי־נָפַל פַּחְדָּם עַל־כָּל־הָעַמִּים: ³ וְכָל־שָׂרֵי הַמְּדִינוֹת וְהָאֲחַשְׁדַּרְפְּנִים וְהַפַּחוֹת וְעֹשֵׂי הַמְּלָאכָה אֲשֶׁר לַמֶּלֶךְ מְנַשְּׂאִים אֶת־הַיְּהוּדִים כִּי־נָפַל פַּחַד־מָרְדֳּכַי עֲלֵיהֶם: ⁴ כִּי־גָדוֹל מָרְדֳּכַי בְּבֵית הַמֶּלֶךְ וְשָׁמְעוֹ הוֹלֵךְ בְּכָל־הַמְּדִינוֹת כִּי־הָאִישׁ מָרְדֳּכַי הוֹלֵךְ וְגָדוֹל: פ ⁵ וַיַּכּוּ הַיְּהוּדִים בְּכָל־אֹיְבֵיהֶם מַכַּת־חֶרֶב וְהֶרֶג וְאַבְדָן וַיַּעֲשׂוּ בְשֹׂנְאֵיהֶם כִּרְצוֹנָם: ⁶ וּבְשׁוּשַׁן הַבִּירָה הָרְגוּ הַיְּהוּדִים וְאַבֵּד חֲמֵשׁ מֵאוֹת אִישׁ: ⁷ וְאֵת פַּרְשַׁנְדָּתָא וְאֵת דַּלְפוֹן וְאֵת אַסְפָּתָא: ⁸ וְאֵת פּוֹרָתָא וְאֵת אֲדַלְיָא וְאֵת אֲרִידָתָא: ⁹ וְאֵת פַּרְמַשְׁתָּא וְאֵת אֲרִיסַי וְאֵת אֲרִדַי וְאֵת וַיְזָתָא: ¹⁰ עֲשֶׂרֶת בְּנֵי הָמָן בֶּן־הַמְּדָתָא צֹרֵר הַיְּהוּדִים הָרָגוּ וּבַבִּזָּה לֹא שָׁלְחוּ אֶת־יָדָם: ¹¹ בַּיּוֹם הַהוּא בָּא מִסְפַּר הַהֲרוּגִים בְּשׁוּשַׁן הַבִּירָה לִפְנֵי הַמֶּלֶךְ: ס ¹² וַיֹּאמֶר הַמֶּלֶךְ לְאֶסְתֵּר הַמַּלְכָּה בְּשׁוּשַׁן הַבִּירָה הָרְגוּ הַיְּהוּדִים וְאַבֵּד חֲמֵשׁ מֵאוֹת אִישׁ וְאֵת עֲשֶׂרֶת בְּנֵי־הָמָן בִּשְׁאָר מְדִינוֹת

¹⁰ the ten sons of Haman the son of Hammedatha, the Jews' enemy; but they did not lay their hands on the plunder.

¹¹ On that day the number of those who were killed at the citadel in Susa was reported to the king.

¹² The king said to Queen Esther, "The Jews have killed and destroyed five hundred men and the ten sons of Haman at the citadel in Susa. What then have they done in the rest of the king's provinces! Now what is your petition? It shall even be granted you. And what is your further request? It shall also be done."

¹³ Then said Esther, "If it pleases the king, let tomorrow also be granted to the Jews who are in Susa to do according to the edict of today; and let Haman's ten sons be hanged on the gallows."

¹⁴ So the king commanded that it should be done so; and an edict was issued in Susa, and Haman's ten sons were hanged.

¹⁵ The Jews who were in Susa assembled also on the fourteenth day of the month Adar and killed three hundred men in Susa, but they did not lay their hands on the plunder.

¹⁶ Now the rest of the Jews who *were* in the king's provinces assembled, to defend their lives and rid themselves of their enemies, and kill 75,000 of those who hated them; but they did not lay their hands on the plunder.

¹⁷ *This was done* on the thirteenth day of the month Adar, and on the fourteenth day they rested and made it a day of feasting and rejoicing.

¹⁸ But the Jews who were in Susa assembled on the thirteenth and the fourteenth of the same month, and they

הַמֶּ֣לֶךְ מֶ֣ה עָשׂ֞וּ וּמַה־שְּׁאֵֽלָתֵךְ֙ וְיִנָּ֣תֵֽן לָ֔ךְ וּמַה־בַּקָּשָׁתֵ֥ךְ ע֖וֹד וְתֵעָֽשׂ׃

¹³ וַתֹּ֣אמֶר אֶסְתֵּ֗ר אִם־עַל־הַמֶּ֨לֶךְ֙ ט֔וֹב יִנָּתֵ֣ן גַּם־מָחָ֗ר לַיְּהוּדִים֙ אֲשֶׁ֣ר בְּשׁוּשָׁ֔ן לַעֲשׂ֖וֹת כְּדָ֣ת הַיּ֑וֹם וְאֵ֛ת עֲשֶׂ֥רֶת בְּנֵֽי־הָמָ֖ן יִתְל֥וּ עַל־הָעֵֽץ׃

¹⁴ וַיֹּ֤אמֶר הַמֶּ֙לֶךְ֙ לְהֵעָ֣שׂוֹת כֵּ֔ן וַתִּנָּתֵ֥ן דָּ֖ת בְּשׁוּשָׁ֑ן וְאֵ֛ת עֲשֶׂ֥רֶת בְּנֵֽי־הָמָ֖ן תָּלֽוּ׃

¹⁵ וַיִּקָּהֲל֞וּ (הַיְּהוּדִיִּם) [הַיְּהוּדִ֤ים] אֲשֶׁר־בְּשׁוּשָׁ֜ן גַּ֣ם בְּי֣וֹם אַרְבָּעָ֤ה עָשָׂר֙ לְחֹ֣דֶשׁ אֲדָ֔ר וַיַּֽהַרְג֣וּ בְשׁוּשָׁ֔ן שְׁלֹ֥שׁ מֵא֖וֹת אִ֑ישׁ וּבַ֨בִּזָּ֔ה לֹ֥א שָׁלְח֖וּ אֶת־יָדָֽם׃

¹⁶ וּשְׁאָ֣ר הַיְּהוּדִ֡ים אֲשֶׁר֩ בִּמְדִינ֨וֹת הַמֶּ֜לֶךְ נִקְהֲל֣וּ ׀ וְעָמֹ֣ד עַל־נַפְשָׁ֗ם וְנ֙וֹחַ֙ מֵאֹ֣יְבֵיהֶ֔ם וְהָרֹג֙ בְּשֹֽׂנְאֵיהֶ֔ם חֲמִשָּׁ֥ה וְשִׁבְעִ֖ים אָ֑לֶף וּבַ֨בִּזָּ֔ה לֹ֥א שָֽׁלְח֖וּ אֶת־יָדָֽם׃

¹⁷ בְּיוֹם־שְׁלֹשָׁ֥ה עָשָׂ֖ר לְחֹ֣דֶשׁ אֲדָ֑ר וְנ֗וֹחַ בְּאַרְבָּעָ֤ה עָשָׂר֙ בּ֔וֹ וְעָשֹׂ֣ה אֹת֔וֹ י֖וֹם מִשְׁתֶּ֥ה וְשִׂמְחָֽה׃

¹⁸ (וְהַיְּהוּדִיִּים) [וְהַיְּהוּדִ֣ים] אֲשֶׁר־בְּשׁוּשָׁ֗ן נִקְהֲלוּ֙ בִּשְׁלֹשָׁ֤ה עָשָׂר֙ בּ֔וֹ וּבְאַרְבָּעָ֥ה עָשָׂ֖ר בּ֑וֹ וְנ֗וֹחַ בַּחֲמִשָּׁ֤ה עָשָׂר֙ בּ֔וֹ וְעָשֹׂ֣ה אֹת֔וֹ י֖וֹם מִשְׁתֶּ֥ה וְשִׂמְחָֽה׃

¹⁹ עַל־כֵּ֞ן הַיְּהוּדִ֣ים (הַפְּרוֹזִים) [הַפְּרָזִ֗ים] הַיֹּשְׁבִים֮ בְּעָרֵ֣י הַפְּרָזוֹת֒ עֹשִׂ֗ים אֵ֠ת י֣וֹם אַרְבָּעָ֤ה עָשָׂר֙ לְחֹ֣דֶשׁ אֲדָ֔ר שִׂמְחָ֥ה וּמִשְׁתֶּ֖ה וְי֣וֹם ט֑וֹב וּמִשְׁל֥וֹחַ מָנ֖וֹת אִ֥ישׁ לְרֵעֵֽהוּ׃ פ

²⁰ וַיִּכְתֹּ֣ב מָרְדֳּכַ֔י אֶת־הַדְּבָרִ֖ים הָאֵ֑לֶּה וַיִּשְׁלַ֨ח סְפָרִ֜ים אֶל־כָּל־הַיְּהוּדִ֗ים אֲשֶׁר֙ בְּכָל־מְדִינוֹת֙ הַמֶּ֣לֶךְ אֲחַשְׁוֵר֔וֹשׁ הַקְּרוֹבִ֖ים וְהָרְחוֹקִֽים׃

²¹ לְקַיֵּם֙ עֲלֵיהֶ֔ם לִהְי֣וֹת עֹשִׂ֗ים אֵ֠ת י֣וֹם אַרְבָּעָ֤ה עָשָׂר֙ לְחֹ֣דֶשׁ אֲדָ֔ר וְאֵ֛ת יוֹם־חֲמִשָּׁ֥ה עָשָׂ֖ר בּ֑וֹ בְּכָל־שָׁנָ֖ה וְשָׁנָֽה׃

²² כַּיָּמִ֗ים אֲשֶׁר־נָ֨חוּ בָהֶ֤ם הַיְּהוּדִים֙ מֵא֣וֹיְבֵיהֶ֔ם וְהַחֹ֗דֶשׁ אֲשֶׁר֩ נֶהְפַּ֨ךְ לָהֶ֤ם מִיָּגוֹן֙ לְשִׂמְחָ֔ה וּמֵאֵ֖בֶל לְי֣וֹם ט֑וֹב לַעֲשׂ֣וֹת אוֹתָ֗ם יְמֵ֞י מִשְׁתֶּ֣ה וְשִׂמְחָ֔ה וּמִשְׁל֤וֹחַ מָנוֹת֙ אִ֣ישׁ לְרֵעֵ֔הוּ וּמַתָּנ֖וֹת לָֽאֶבְיוֹנִֽים׃

²³ וְקִבֵּל֙ הַיְּהוּדִ֔ים אֵ֥ת אֲשֶׁר־הֵחֵ֖לּוּ לַעֲשׂ֑וֹת וְאֵ֛ת אֲשֶׁר־כָּתַ֥ב מָרְדֳּכַ֖י אֲלֵיהֶֽם׃

rested on the fifteenth day and made it a day of feasting and rejoicing.

19 Therefore the Jews of the rural areas, who live in the rural towns, make the fourteenth day of the month Adar *a* holiday for rejoicing and feasting and sending portions *of food* to one another.

20 Then Mordecai recorded these events, and he sent letters to all the Jews who were in all the provinces of King Ahasuerus, both near and far,

21 obliging them to celebrate the fourteenth day of the month Adar, and the fifteenth day of the same month, annually,

22 because on those days the Jews rid themselves of their enemies, and *it was a* month which was turned for them from sorrow into gladness and from mourning into a holiday; that they should make them days of feasting and rejoicing and sending portions *of food* to one another and gifts to the poor.

23 Thus the Jews undertook what they had started to do, and what Mordecai had written to them.

24 For Haman the son of Hammedatha, the Agagite, the adversary of all the Jews, had schemed against the Jews to destroy them and had cast Pur, that is the lot, to disturb them and destroy them.

25 But when it came to the king's attention, he commanded by letter that his wicked scheme which he had devised against the Jews, should return on his own head and that he and his sons should be hanged on the gallows.

26 Therefore they called these days Purim after the name of Pur. And because of the instructions in this letter, both what they

24 כִּי הָמָן בֶּן־הַמְּדָתָא הָאֲגָגִי צֹרֵר כָּל־הַיְּהוּדִים חָשַׁב עַל־הַיְּהוּדִים לְאַבְּדָם וְהִפִּיל פּוּר הוּא הַגּוֹרָל לְהֻמָּם וּלְאַבְּדָם׃

25 וּבְבֹאָהּ לִפְנֵי הַמֶּלֶךְ אָמַר עִם־הַסֵּפֶר יָשׁוּב מַחֲשַׁבְתּוֹ הָרָעָה אֲשֶׁר־חָשַׁב עַל־הַיְּהוּדִים עַל־רֹאשׁוֹ וְתָלוּ אֹתוֹ וְאֶת־בָּנָיו עַל־הָעֵץ׃

26 עַל־כֵּן קָרְאוּ לַיָּמִים הָאֵלֶּה פוּרִים עַל־שֵׁם הַפּוּר עַל־כֵּן עַל־כָּל־דִּבְרֵי הָאִגֶּרֶת הַזֹּאת וּמָה־רָאוּ עַל־כָּכָה וּמָה הִגִּיעַ אֲלֵיהֶם׃

27 קִיְּמוּ (וְקִבֵּל) [וְקִבְּלוּ] הַיְּהוּדִים עֲלֵיהֶם וְעַל־זַרְעָם וְעַל כָּל־הַנִּלְוִים עֲלֵיהֶם וְלֹא יַעֲבוֹר לִהְיוֹת עֹשִׂים אֵת שְׁנֵי הַיָּמִים הָאֵלֶּה כִּכְתָבָם וְכִזְמַנָּם בְּכָל־שָׁנָה וְשָׁנָה׃

28 וְהַיָּמִים הָאֵלֶּה נִזְכָּרִים וְנַעֲשִׂים בְּכָל־דּוֹר וָדוֹר מִשְׁפָּחָה וּמִשְׁפָּחָה מְדִינָה וּמְדִינָה וְעִיר וָעִיר וִימֵי הַפּוּרִים הָאֵלֶּה לֹא יַעַבְרוּ מִתּוֹךְ הַיְּהוּדִים וְזִכְרָם לֹא־יָסוּף מִזַּרְעָם׃ ס

29 וַתִּכְתֹּב אֶסְתֵּר הַמַּלְכָּה בַת־אֲבִיחַיִל וּמָרְדֳּכַי הַיְּהוּדִי אֶת־כָּל־תֹּקֶף לְקַיֵּם אֵת אִגֶּרֶת הַפֻּרִים הַזֹּאת הַשֵּׁנִית׃

30 וַיִּשְׁלַח סְפָרִים אֶל־כָּל־הַיְּהוּדִים אֶל־שֶׁבַע וְעֶשְׂרִים וּמֵאָה מְדִינָה מַלְכוּת אֲחַשְׁוֵרוֹשׁ דִּבְרֵי שָׁלוֹם וֶאֱמֶת׃

31 לְקַיֵּם אֶת־יְמֵי הַפֻּרִים הָאֵלֶּה בִּזְמַנֵּיהֶם כַּאֲשֶׁר קִיַּם עֲלֵיהֶם מָרְדֳּכַי הַיְּהוּדִי וְאֶסְתֵּר הַמַּלְכָּה וְכַאֲשֶׁר קִיְּמוּ עַל־נַפְשָׁם וְעַל־זַרְעָם דִּבְרֵי הַצֹּמוֹת וְזַעֲקָתָם׃

32 וּמַאֲמַר אֶסְתֵּר קִיַּם דִּבְרֵי הַפֻּרִים הָאֵלֶּה וְנִכְתָּב בַּסֵּפֶר׃ פ

had seen in this regard and what had happened to them,

²⁷ the Jews established and made a custom for themselves and for their descendants and for all those who allied themselves with them, so that they would not fail to celebrate these two days according to their regulation and according to their appointed time annually.

²⁸ So these days were to be remembered and celebrated throughout every generation, every family, every province and every city; and these days of Purim were not to fail from among the Jews, or their memory fade from their descendants.

²⁹ Then Queen Esther, daughter of Abihail, with Mordecai the Jew, wrote with full authority to confirm this second letter about Purim.

³⁰ He sent letters to all the Jews, to the 127 provinces of the kingdom of Ahasuerus, *namely*, words of peace and truth,

³¹ to establish these days of Purim at their appointed times, just as Mordecai the Jew and Queen Esther had established for them, and just as they had established for themselves and for their descendants with instructions for their times of fasting and their lamentations.

³² The command of Esther established these customs for Purim, and it was written in the book.

Process of Discovery

Linguistics Section

Linguistic Structure

A [1] Now in the twelfth month (that is, the month Adar), on the thirteenth day when the king's command and edict were about to be executed, on the day when the enemies of the Jews hoped to gain the mastery over them, it was turned to the contrary so that the Jews themselves gained the mastery over those who hated them. [2] The Jews assembled in their cities throughout all the provinces of King Ahasuerus to lay hands on those who sought their harm; and no one could stand before them, for the dread of them had fallen on all the peoples. [3] Even all the princes of the provinces, the satraps, the governors and those who were doing the king's business assisted the Jews, because the dread of Mordecai had fallen on them. [4] Indeed, Mordecai was great in the king's house, and his fame spread throughout all the provinces; for the man Mordecai became greater and greater.

B [5] Thus the Jews struck all their enemies with the sword, killing and destroying; and they did what they pleased to those who hated them. [6] At the citadel in Susa the Jews killed and destroyed five hundred men, [7] and Parshandatha, Dalphon, Aspatha, [8] Poratha, Adalia, Aridatha, [9] Parmashta, Arisai, Aridai and Vaizatha, [10] the ten sons of Haman the son of Hammedatha, the Jews' enemy; but they did not lay their hands on the plunder.

C [11] On that day the number of those who were killed at the citadel in Susa was reported to the king. [12] The king said to Queen Esther, "The Jews have killed and destroyed five hundred men and the ten sons of Haman at the citadel in Susa. What then have they done in the rest of the king's provinces! Now what is your petition? It shall even be granted you. And what is your further request? It shall also be done." [13] Then said Esther, "If it pleases the king, let tomorrow also be granted to the Jews who are in Susa to do according to the edict of today; and let Haman's ten sons be hanged on the gallows." [14] So the king commanded that it should be done so; and an edict was issued in Susa, and Haman's ten sons were hanged.

B' ¹⁵ The Jews who were in Susa assembled also on the fourteenth day of the month Adar and killed three hundred men in Susa, but they did not lay their hands on the plunder. ¹⁶ Now the rest of the Jews who *were* in the king's provinces assembled, to defend their lives and rid themselves of their enemies, and kill 75,000 of those who hated them; but they did not lay their hands on the plunder.

A' ¹⁷ *This was done* on the thirteenth day of the month Adar, and on the fourteenth day they rested and made it a day of feasting and rejoicing. ¹⁸ But the Jews who were in Susa assembled on the thirteenth and the fourteenth of the same month, and they rested on the fifteenth day and made it a day of feasting and rejoicing. ¹⁹ Therefore the Jews of the rural areas, who live in the rural towns, make the fourteenth day of the month Adar *a* holiday for rejoicing and feasting and sending portions *of food* to one another.

A ²⁰ Then Mordecai recorded these events, and he sent letters to all the Jews who were in all the provinces of King Ahasuerus, both near and far, ²¹ obliging them to celebrate the fourteenth day of the month Adar, and the fifteenth day of the same month, annually, ²² because on those days the Jews rid themselves of their enemies, and *it was a* month which was turned for them from sorrow into gladness and from mourning into a holiday; that they should make them days of feasting and rejoicing and sending portions *of food* to one another and gifts to the poor.

> **B** ²³ Thus the Jews undertook what they had started to do, and what Mordecai had written to them.

> > **C** ²⁴ For Haman the son of Hammedatha, the Agagite, the adversary of all the Jews, had schemed against the Jews to destroy them and had cast Pur, that is the lot, to disturb them and destroy them. ²⁵ But when it came to the king's attention, he commanded by letter that his wicked scheme which he had devised against the Jews, should return on his own head and that he and his sons should be hanged on the gallows. ²⁶ Therefore they called these days Purim after the name of Pur.

> > **B'** And because of the instructions in this letter, both what they had seen in this regard and what had happened to them, ²⁷ the Jews established and made a custom for themselves and for their descendants and for all those who allied themselves with them, so that they would not fail to celebrate these two days

according to their regulation and according to their appointed time annually. [28] So these days were to be remembered and celebrated throughout every generation, every family, every province and every city; and these days of Purim were not to fail from among the Jews, or their memory fade from their descendants.

A' [29] Then Queen Esther, daughter of Abihail, with Mordecai the Jew, wrote with full authority to confirm this second letter about Purim. [30] He sent letters to all the Jews, to the 127 provinces of the kingdom of Ahasuerus, *namely*, words of peace and truth, [31] to establish these days of Purim at their appointed times, just as Mordecai the Jew and Queen Esther had established for them, and just as they had established for themselves and for their descendants with instructions for their times of fasting and their lamentations. [32] The command of Esther established these customs for Purim, and it was written in the book.

Discussion

This chapter consists of two chiasms. The first chiasm tells the story of the destruction of the enemies of the Jews. The second chiasm is about the inauguration of the holiday of Purim.

Additional Information from the Targums

The Targum Rishon in verse thirteen says that Haman and his ten sons were hung three cubits apart from each other (about 8 feet). Zeresh, Haman's wife, fled Susa with her seventy children, and they became beggars going door to door.[64]

---

[64] "The Aramaic Bible, the Two Targums of Esther" The Liturgical Press. 1991

The Holiday Purim

"Why Is It Called Purim?

Purim means "lots" in ancient Persian. The holiday was thus named since Haman had thrown lots to determine when he would carry out his diabolical scheme. You can pronounce this name many ways. In Eastern tradition, it is called poo-REEM. Among Westerners, it is often called PUH-rim. Some Central-European communities even call it PEE-rim. (WARNING: Calling this holiday PYOO-rim—as English speakers are sometimes wont to do—is a surefire newbie cover-blower.)

Purim Observances

- Reading of the Megillah (book of Esther), which recounts the story of the Purim miracle. This is done once on the eve of Purim and then again on the following day.
- Giving money gifts to at least two poor people.
- Sending gifts of two kinds of food to at least one person.
- A festive Purim feast, which often includes wine or other intoxicating beverages.

Purim Customs

There is a spirit of liveliness and fun on Purim that is unparalleled on the Jewish calendar. If there were ever a day to "let loose" and just be Jewish, this is it!

It is also customary for children (and adults, if they desire) to dress up in costumes.

A traditional Purim food is *hamantaschen* (or *oznay Haman),* three-cornered pastries bursting with poppy seeds or another sweet filling.

On the day before Purim (or on the Thursday before, when Purim is on Sunday), it is customary to fast, commemorating Esther's fasting and praying to G-d that He save His people.

When to Celebrate

One of the unique aspects of Purim is the diverse timing for its celebration.

● Common Custom: Jews all over the world celebrate Purim on Adar 14, the day when our ancestors rested from the war against their enemies.

● Walled Cities: Since the Jews of Shushan rested one day later, their Purim was deferred to the 15th. This was extended to include any city that was surrounded by walls in the days of Joshua, notably Jerusalem.

● Small Towns: In ancient times, villagers only banded together with fellow Jews in the larger towns on Mondays and Thursdays, which were market days. Thus, the sages decreed that they should read the Megillah on the market day preceding 14 Adar. This custom is no longer practiced."[65]

---

[65] Chabad.org, "What Is Purim?," Judaism, March 7, 2008, Accessed December 13, 2019, https://www.chabad.org/holidays/purim/article_cdo/aid/645309/jewish/What-Is-Purim.htm.

Thoughts

The enemies of the LORD's people were destroyed through the courage of Esther. You must ask yourself if you are that faithful to the LORD that you would be willing to do something similar to Esther. When you see injustice occurring to the LORD's people, will you step in and try to do something about it?

Chapter Ten

Language

New American Standard 1995	Hebrew
[1] Now King Ahasuerus laid a tribute on the land and on the coastlands of the sea. [2] And all the accomplishments of his authority and strength, and the full account of the greatness of Mordecai to which the king advanced him, are they not written in the Book of the Chronicles of the Kings of Media and Persia? [3] For Mordecai the Jew was second *only* to King Ahasuerus, and great among the Jews and in favor with his many kinsmen, one who sought the good of his people and one who spoke for the welfare of his whole nation.	וַיָּשֶׂם הַמֶּלֶךְ (אֲחַשְׁרֹשׁ) [אֲחַשְׁוֵרוֹשׁ] מַס עַל־הָאָרֶץ וְאִיֵּי הַיָּם: [2] וְכָל־מַעֲשֵׂה תׇקְפּוֹ וּגְבוּרָתוֹ וּפָרָשַׁת גְּדֻלַּת מׇרְדֳּכַי אֲשֶׁר גִּדְּלוֹ הַמֶּלֶךְ הֲלוֹא־הֵם כְּתוּבִים עַל־סֵפֶר דִּבְרֵי הַיָּמִים לְמַלְכֵי מָדַי וּפָרָס: [3] כִּי מׇרְדֳּכַי הַיְּהוּדִי מִשְׁנֶה לַמֶּלֶךְ אֲחַשְׁוֵרוֹשׁ וְגָדוֹל לַיְּהוּדִים וְרָצוּי לְרֹב אֶחָיו דֹּרֵשׁ טוֹב לְעַמּוֹ וְדֹבֵר שָׁלוֹם לְכָל־זַרְעוֹ:

Process of Discovery

Linguistics Section

Linguistic Structure

[Conclusion] [1] Now King Ahasuerus laid a tribute on the land and on the coastlands of the sea. [2] And all the accomplishments of his authority and strength, and the full account of the greatness of Mordecai to which the king advanced him, are they not written in the Book of the Chronicles of the Kings of Media and Persia? [3] For Mordecai the Jew was second *only* to King Ahasuerus, and great among the Jews and in favor with his many kinsmen, one who sought the good of his people and one who spoke for the welfare of his whole nation.

Discussion

This short chapter tells the reader that Mordecai became second to King Ahasuerus of Persia.

Thoughts

The Jewish people were taken into captivity by the Babylonians. While in Babylon, Jews like Daniel and his brothers were able to rise to high political positions in the Empire. In the Persian Empire, the Jew Mordecai was able to rise to a high position. Even in captivity, the Jews were respected as the children of the LORD.

Bibliography

n.d. *A Throw of Dice*. Accessed November 11, 2019. https://www.chabad.org/holidays/purim/article_cdo/aid/1404/jewish/A-Throw-of-Dice.htm.

n.d. *Ahasuerus*. Accessed November 5, 2019. https://www.jewishvirtuallibrary.org/ahasuerus.

n.d. *Ancient Jewish History, the Amalekites*. Accessed November 19, 2019. https://www.jewishvirtuallibrary.org/the-amalekites.

Berlin, A. 2001. *Esther*. Philadephia, PA: Jewish Publication Society.

Bush, F.W. 1996. *Ruth, Esther (volume 1) the WORD Commentary*. Dallas, TX: Word Incorporated.

Davis, Anne Kimball. 2012. *The Synoptic Gospels*.

Lamsa, Rocco A. Errico and George M. 2010. *Aramaic Light on Ezra through the Song of Solomon*. Smyma, GA: Noohra Foundation.

Levene, Osher Chaim and Yehoshua Hartman. 2013. *Jewish Wisdom in the Numbers*. Brooklyn, NY: Mesorah Publications.

Mark, Joshua J. n.d. *Ancient History Encyclopedia*. Accessed November 2, 2019. https://www.ancient.eu/susa/.

1986. *Back to School*. Directed by Paper Clip Productions.

Tauber, Yanki. n.d. *A Throw of Dice*. Accessed February 29, 2000. https://www.chabad.org/holidays/purim/article_cdo/aid/1404/jewish/A-Throw-of-Dice.htm.

1991. *The Aramaic Bible: the two targums of Esther*. Liturgical Press.

2008. *What is Purim?* March 7. Accessed December 13, 2019.
https://www.chabad.org/holidays/purim/article_cdo/aid/645309/jewish/What-Is-Purim.htm.